B. P. Pratten

Syriac Documents attributed to the first three Centuries

B. P. Pratten

Syriac Documents attributed to the first three Centuries

ISBN/EAN: 9783337240202

Printed in Europe, USA, Canada, Australia, Japan

Cover: Foto ©ninafisch / pixelio.de

More available books at **www.hansebooks.com**

SYRIAC DOCUMENTS

ATTRIBUTED TO

THE FIRST THREE CENTURIES

Translated by

REV. B. P. PRATTEN, B.A.

EDINBURGH:
T. & T. CLARK, 38, GEORGE STREET.
MDCCCLXXI.

CONTENTS.

	PAGE
INTRODUCTORY NOTICE BY THE TRANSLATOR,	1

FROM THE HISTORY OF THE CHURCH.

Story concerning the King of Edessa,	5
The Teaching of Addæus the Apostle,	12
The Teaching of the Apostles,	35
The Teaching of Simon Cephas in the City of Rome,	49
Acts of Sharbil,	56
Martyrdom of Barsamya,	80
Martyrdom of Habib the Deacon,	91
Homily on Habib the Martyr, by Mar Jacob,	105
Homily on Guria and Shamuna, by Mar Jacob,	117
Canticle of Mar Jacob on Edessa,	129
Extracts from various Books concerning Abgar the King and Addæus the Apostle,	131

APPENDIX.

Martyrdom of the Holy Confessors Shamuna, Guria, and Habib,	136
Moses of Chorene: History of Armenia,	150

INDEXES,—
Index of Texts,	165
Index of Subjects,	165

ANCIENT SYRIAC DOCUMENTS.

INTRODUCTORY NOTICE BY THE TRANSLATOR.

THESE Documents were selected by the late Dr. Cureton, from manuscripts acquired by the British Museum from the Nitrian Monastery in Lower Egypt, of which the first portion arrived in 1841, the second in 1843, and a third in 1847. The preparation of them for publication occupied the closing days of his life. It is to be regretted that his death occurred before he was able to write a preface: the more so because, to use the words of Dr. W. Wright, the editor of the posthumous work, "he had studied the questions connected with this volume for years and from every point of view." In a note occurring in the preface to his *Festal Letters of Athanasius*, p. xxiii, he says: "I have found among the Syriac MSS. in the British Museum a considerable portion of the original Aramaic document which Eusebius cites as preserved in the archives of Edessa, and various passages from it quoted by several authors, with other testimonies which seem to be sufficient to establish the fact of the early conversion of the inhabitants of that city, and among them of the king himself, although his successors afterwards relapsed into paganism. These, together with accounts of the martyrdom of some of the first bishops of that city, forming a most interesting accession to our knowledge of the early propagation of Christianity in the East down to about A.D. 300, I have already transcribed, and hope to publish." "He was himself firmly persuaded," adds Dr. Wright, "of the genuineness of the

Epistles attributed to Abgar, king of Edessa, and our Lord: an opinion which he shared with such illustrious scholars as Baronius, Tillemont, Cave, R. Mountague (Bishop of Norwich), and Grabe."

Without attempting here to decide what degree of historical value belongs to these Documents, it may be proper to observe that the several matters contained in them are so far distinct from one another that they do not necessarily stand or fall together. Such matters are: the celebrated Epistles, the conversion of King Abgar Uchomo, the visit of Thaddæus, and the early prevalence of Christianity at Edessa. With regard to the letters said to have passed between Abgar and our Lord, it seems sufficient, without referring to the internal evidence, to remark, with Lardner and Neander, that it is inconceivable how anything written by Christ should have remained down to the time of Eusebius unknown to the rest of the world.[1] The conversion of Abgar is a distinct matter of inquiry. But on this again, doubt, to say the least, is cast by the statement that Abgar Bar Manu, who reigned between the years 160 and 170 A.D., is the first king of Edessa on whose coins the usual symbols of the Baal-worship of the country are wanting, these being replaced in his case by the sign of the Cross.[2] If this refers to a complete series of the coins of Edessa, the evidence afforded must be considered very strong. For although, to take a parallel instance, "we seek in vain for Christian emblems on the coinage of Constantine, the first Christian emperor,"[3] this may readily be accounted for by his preference of military distinction to the humbler honours conferred by his new faith, whilst it does not appear that *anti*-Christian emblems are found, and on the coins of his son and successor Christian emblems do make their appearance. The other two subjects referred to do not lie under the same suspicion. There is nothing in the nature of the case to disprove the visit of Thaddæus (or Addæus)—nothing improbable in the fact itself, whatever

---

[1] *Hist. of the Church*, vol. i. p. 109 (For. Theol. Lib.).
[2] Bayer, *Historia Edessena e nummis illustrata*, l. iii. p. 173.
[3] Humphreys' *Coin-Collector's Manual*, p. 364.

judgment may be formed of the details of it presented to us here. If, however, the visit of Thaddæus also should have to be ranked among apocryphal stories, this would not affect the remaining point—that with which we are chiefly concerned in these Documents. "It is certain," says Neander, "that Christianity was early diffused in this country." How early, is not so certain. But the evidence furnished by the later portions of these Documents, which there is nothing to contradict and much to confirm, proves that early in the second century Christianity had already made many converts there. The martyrdoms of Sharbil and Barsamya are said to have occurred A.D. 113 (it should have been 115), the year in which Trajan conquered the Parthian kingdom, of which Edessa was a part; and, whilst the pagan element was plainly predominant, we find the Christians sufficiently numerous to have a bishop and presbyters and deacons. This sufficiently falls in with the proof already adduced of the conversion of even a king of Edessa about fifty years later.

To the Documents which are presumably of the ante-Nicene age, Dr. Cureton added two Metrical Homilies by Jacob of Serug, who lived in the next century. But, as they are so closely connected with the most interesting portions of the rest, the martyrdoms, and are besides of considerable merit as compositions, the decision of the editors to insert them will, it is presumed, be approved by most readers. The two supplemental portions, one from the Latin of Simeon Metaphrastes, and the other from Le Vaillant de Florival's French translation of Moses of Chorene, have also been inserted.

The translation of the Syriac portions, although made with Dr. Cureton's version constantly in sight, may fairly be considered as independent. The only matter in which his authority has been relied on is the supply of the necessary vowels, for the text is vowelless, in the case of proper names; and even to this one exception occurs, in the *Martyrdom of Barsamya*, where "Evaristus" has been adopted instead of his "Erastus." In regard to the sense, it has been frequently found necessary to differ from him, while a style somewhat freer, though, it is hoped, not less faithful, has been employed. The Metrical Homilies also have been arranged so as to present the appearance of poetry. The results of Dr. Wright's collation of the text with the MSS. have also contributed to the greater correctness of the work.

The translator desires very thankfully to acknowledge his obligations to Dr. R. Payne Smith, Regius Professor of Divinity in the University of Oxford,[1] the progress of whose *Thesaurus Syriacus* is regarded with so much satisfaction and hope, for his kindness in furnishing much valuable information respecting matters on which the lexicons are silent.

The notes in square brackets are by the translator. The others, where the contrary is not indicated, are, at least in substance, Dr. Cureton's: though their citation does not always imply approval.

[The translator takes the opportunity of correcting the error by which the preparation of Tatian's work in vol. iii. of this Series was ascribed to him. The credit of it is due in the first instance to his lamented friend Mr. J. E. Ryland, at whose request, and subsequently by that of the editors, he undertook to correct the manuscript, but was soon obliged by other engagements to relinquish the task.]

[1] Now Dean of Canterbury.

ANCIENT SYRIAC DOCUMENTS

RELATING TO

THE EARLIEST ESTABLISHMENT OF CHRISTIANITY IN
EDESSA AND THE NEIGHBOURING COUNTRIES.

FROM THE HISTORY OF THE CHURCH.

[BY EUSEBIUS OF CÆSAREA.]

[BOOK I. CHAPTER] THE THIRTEENTH.[1]

STORY CONCERNING THE KING OF EDESSA.[2]

NOW the story relating to Thaddæus was on this wise :—

When the Godhead of our Saviour and Lord Jesus Christ was being proclaimed among all men by reason of the astonishing mighty-works which He wrought, and myriads, even from countries remote from the land of Judæa, who were afflicted with sicknesses and diseases of every kind, were coming to Him in the hope of being healed, King Abgar[3] also, who was renowned among the

---

[1] The MS. from which this extract from Eusebius is taken is numbered 14,639, fol. 15 b. It is described in Cureton's *Corpus Ignatianum*, p. 350.

[2] [Properly *Urrhoi*, or *Orrhoi* (ܐܘܪܗܝ). It seems probable that the word is connected with Osrhoene, the name of the province in which Edessa held an important place, the correct form of which is supposed to be *Orrhoene*. The name *Edessa* (ܐܕܣܐ) occurs only once in these Documents, viz. in the "*Acts of Sharbil*," *sub init.*]

[3] "By this title all the toparchs of Edessa were called, just as the Roman emperors were called Cæsars, the kings of Egypt Pharaohs or Ptolemies, the kings of Syria Antiochi." Assem. *Bibl. Or.* vol. i. p. 261. Assemani adds: "Abgar in Syriac means *lame*." Moses of Chorene, however, with more probability, derives it from the Armenian *Avag-aïr*, "grand homme, à cause de sa grande mansuétude et de sa sagesse, et, de plus, à cause de sa taille." See below the extract from his *History of Armenia*, Book ii. ch. 26.

5

nations on the east of the Euphrates for his valour, had his body wasting away with a grievous disease, such as there is no cure for among men. And when he heard and was informed of the name of Jesus, and about the mighty works which He did (for every one alike bore witness concerning Him), he sent a letter of request by a man belonging to him,[1] and besought Him to come and heal him of his disease.

But our Saviour at the time that he asked Him did not comply with his request. Yet He deigned to give him[2] a letter [in reply]: for He promised him that He would send one of His disciples, and heal his sicknesses, and give salvation[3] to him and to all who were connected with him.[4] Nor did He delay to fulfil His promise to him: but after He was risen from the place of the dead, and was received into heaven, Thomas[5] the apostle, one of the twelve, as by an impulse from God, sent Thaddæus,[6] who was himself also numbered among the seventy[7] disciples of Christ, to Edessa, to be a preacher and proclaimer of the teaching of Christ; and the promise of Christ was through him fulfilled.

Thou hast in writing the evidence of these things, which is taken from the Book of Records[8] which was at Edessa: for at that time the kingdom was still standing.[9] In the

---

[1] Eusebius has δι' ἐπιστολχφόρου. [See note on ταχυδρόμου, on next page.]

[2] [Lit. "deemed him worthy of."]

[3] [Gr. σωτηρίαν: and so the Syriac word, meaning "life," is generally to be translated in this collection.]

[4] Syr. "near to him;" Gr. τῶν προσηκόντων.

[5] His real name was Judas Thomas: see p. 8.

[6] The name is taken from Eusebius, but in the original Syriac treatises, which follow, he is called Addæus.

[7] In *The Teaching of the Apostles* he is said to have been one of the "seventy-two apostles." His name, like that of Thomas, seems to have been the very common one, Judas.

[8] These were kept in the archives of the kingdom, which were transferred by Abgar from Nisibis to Edessa when he made it the capital of his dominions. See Moses Chor. B. ii. ch. 27, *infra*. The archives appear to have been still kept at Edessa in A.D. 550.

[9] The kingdom of Edessa was brought to an end and entirely subjected to the Romans in A.D. 217 or 218.

documents, then, which were [kept] there, in which was contained whatever was done by those of old down to the time of Abgar, these things also are found preserved down to the present hour. There is, however, nothing to prevent our hearing the very letters themselves, which have been taken by us[1] from the archives, and are in words to this effect, translated from Aramaic into Greek.

Copy of the letter which was written by King[2] Abgar to Jesus, and sent to Him by the hand of Hananias,[3] the Tabularius,[4] to Jerusalem:—

"Abgar the Black,[5] sovereign[6] of the country, to Jesus, the good Saviour, who has appeared in the country of Jerusalem: Peace. I have heard about Thee,[7] and about the healing which is wrought by Thy hands without drugs and roots. For, as it is reported, Thou makest the blind to see, and the lame to walk; and Thou cleansest the lepers, and Thou castest out unclean spirits and demons, and Thou healest those who are tormented with lingering diseases, and Thou raisest the dead. And when I heard all these things about Thee, I settled in my mind one of two things: either that Thou art God, who hast come down from

---

[1] The extract from the archives was probably made by Sextus Julius Africanus, and copied by Eusebius from his *Chronographia*.

[2] Gr. τόπαρχος.

[3] Called Hanan in the original Syriac document; and so in Moses Chor.: Eusebius has 'Ανανίας, which is copied here.

[4] Gr. ταχυδρόμου. But the post held by Hananias must have been one of more dignity than that of a *courier*. He was probably a Secretary of State. In *The Acts of Addæus*, p. 35, he is called, in connection with the name Tabularius, a *sharir*, or confidential servant. [It would seem that Tabularius has been confounded with Tabellarius (a letter-carrier).]

[5] Or "Abgar Uchomo." The epithet was peculiar to this King Abgar. He was the fourteenth king: the eleventh was called Abgar Sumoco, or "the Red." [The occasion of the name "Black" is doubtful: it can hardly have arisen from the fact that Abgar was suffering, as Cedrenus asserts, from the black leprosy.]

[6] ["Head," or "chief."]

[7] Comp. Matt. iv. 24: "And His fame went throughout all Syria," etc. See also Moses Chor. B. ii. c. 30.

heaven, and [therefore] doest these things; or that Thou art the Son of God, and [therefore] doest these things. On this account, therefore, I have written to beg of Thee that Thou wouldest weary Thyself to come to me, and heal this disease which I have. [And not only so:] for I have also heard that the Jews murmur against Thee, and wish to do Thee harm. But I have a city, small and beautiful, which is sufficient for two."

Copy of those things which were written[1] by Jesus by the hand of Hananias, the Tabularius, to Abgar, sovereign of the country:—

"Blessed is he that hath believed in me, not having seen me. For it is written concerning me, that those who see me will not believe in me, and that those will believe who have not seen me, and will be saved. But touching that which thou hast written to me, that I should come to thee—it is meet that I should finish here all that for the sake of which I have been sent; and, after I have finished it, then I shall be taken up to Him that sent me; and, when I have been taken up, I will send to thee one of my disciples, that he may heal thy disease, and give salvation to thee and to those who are with thee."

To these letters, moreover, is appended the following also in the Aramaic tongue:—

After Jesus was ascended, Judas Thomas sent to him Thaddæus the apostle, one of the Seventy. And, when he was come, he lodged with Tobias, son of Tobias. And, when the news about him was heard, they made it known to Abgar: "The apostle of Jesus is come hither, as He sent thee word." Thaddæus, moreover, began to heal every disease and sickness by the power of God, so that all men were amazed. And, when Abgar heard the great and marvellous cures which he wrought, he bethought himself that he was the person about whom Jesus had sent him word and said to him: When I have been taken up, I will send to thee one of my disciples, that he may heal thy disease. So he sent and called Tobias, with whom he was lodging, and said to him:

---

[1] Gr. ἀντιγραφέντα, "written in reply."

I have heard that a mighty man has come, and has entered in and taken up his lodging in thy house: bring him up, therefore, to me. And when Tobias came to Thaddæus he said to him: Abgar the king has sent and called me, and commanded me to bring thee up to him, that thou mayest heal him. And Thaddæus said: I will go up, because to him have I been sent with power. Tobias therefore rose up early the next day, and took Thaddæus, and came to Abgar.

Now, when they were come up, his princes happened to be standing[1] there. And immediately, as he was entering in, a great vision appeared to Abgar on the countenance of Thaddæus the apostle. And, when Abgar saw Thaddæus, he prostrated himself before him.[2] And astonishment seized upon all who were standing there: for they had not themselves seen that vision, which appeared to Abgar alone. And he proceeded to ask Thaddæus: Art thou in truth the disciple of Jesus the Son of God, who said to me, I will send to thee one of my disciples, that he may heal thee and give thee salvation? And Thaddæus answered and said: Because thou hast mightily[3] believed on Him that sent me, therefore have I been sent to thee; and again, if thou shalt believe on Him, thou shalt have the requests of thy heart. And Abgar said to him: In such wise have I believed on Him, that I have even desired to take an army and extirpate those Jews who crucified Him; [and had done so], were it not that I was restrained by reason of the dominion of the Romans.[4] And Thaddæus said: Our Lord has fulfilled the will of His Father; and, having fulfilled it, has been taken up to His Father. Abgar said to him: I too

---

[1] [Cureton, " were assembled and standing;" nearly as Euseb.: παρόντων καὶ ἑστώτων. But in 2 Sam. xx. 1, the only reference given by Castel for the word, ܘܩܐܡ is used for the Heb. נקרא, " he chanced."]

[2] [ܣܓܕ, like the προσκύνησις of Eusebius, may be rendered " worshipped."]

[3] [ܪܘܪܒܐܝܬ; Gr. μεγάλως, lit. " greatly ;" C. " nobly." But nothing more than *intensity* is necessarily denoted by either word. Compare, for the Syriac, Ps. cxix. 107, 167 ; Dan. ii. 12.]

[4] Compare the letters of Abgar and Tiberius, p. 26

have believed in Him and in His Father. And[1] Thaddæus said: Therefore do I lay my hand upon thee in His name. And when he had done this, immediately he was healed of his sickness and of the disease which he had. And Abgar marvelled, because, like as he had heard concerning Jesus, so he saw in deeds [wrought] by the hand of Thaddæus His disciple: since without drugs and roots he healed him; and not him only, but also Abdu,[2] son of Abdu, who had the gout: for he too went in, and fell at his feet,[3] and when he prayed over him he was healed. And many other people of their city did he heal, and he did great works, and preached the word of God.

After these things Abgar said to him: Thou, Thaddæus, doest these things by the power of God; we also marvel at them. But in addition to all these things I beg of thee to relate to me the story about the coming of Christ, and in what manner it was; and about His power, and by what power He wrought those things of which I have heard.

And Thaddæus said: For the present I will be silent;[4] but, because I have been sent to preach the word of God, assemble me to-morrow all the people of thy city, and I will preach before them, and sow amongst them the word of life; and [will tell them] about the coming of Christ, how it took place; and about His mission,[5] for what purpose He was sent by His Father; and about His power and His deeds,

---

[1] In the next piece, *The Teaching of Addæus*, i.e. Thaddæus, we have a portion of the original Syriac from which Eusebius' translation was made. The only portions that correspond are: in the present piece, from this place to "— accept that of others," near the end; and, in the following one, from the beginning to "— that which is not ours." Some of the variations are worthy of notice.

[2] See note 1, p. 14.

[3] This answers sufficiently well to the Greek: $ὃς\ καὶ\ αὐτὸς\ προσελθὼν\ ὑπὸ\ τοὺς\ πόδας\ αὐτοῦ\ ἔπεσεν$; but, as the original Syriac, p. 12, reads "he too brought [presented] his feet to him, and he laid his hands upon them and healed him," the Greek translation must have been at fault.

[4] The original Syriac has "I will not hold my peace from declaring this."

[5] So Euseb. The orig. Syr. has "His sender."

and about the mysteries which He spake in the world, and by what power He wrought these things, and about His new preaching,[1] and about His abasement and His humiliation, and how He humbled and emptied and abased Himself, and was crucified, and descended to Hades,[2] and broke through the enclosure[3] which had never been broken through [before], and raised up the dead, and descended alone, and ascended with a great multitude to His Father.[4]

Abgar, therefore, commanded that in the morning all the people of his city should assemble, and hear the preaching of Thaddæus. And afterwards he commanded gold and silver to be given to him; but he received it not, and said: If we have forsaken that which was our own, how shall we accept that of others?

These things were done in the year 340.[5]

In order, moreover, that these things may not have been translated to no purpose word for word from the Aramaic into Greek, they are placed in their order of time here.

[Here] endeth the first book.

---

[1] The orig. Syr. has "the certitude [or, unerring truth] of His preaching." The error seems to have arisen from the Greek translator confounding ܩܘܫܬܐ with ܚܕܬܐ. [More probably with ܚܘܕܬܐ, "newness (of his preaching)," which was freely translated by him (περὶ) τῆς καινῆς αὐτοῦ κηρύξεως; and this, again, was by the Syrian re-translator rendered literally, as in the text.]

[2] Or "Sheol," as in Hebrew. The orig. Syr. gives "the place of the dead."

[3] Eph. ii. 14.   [4] Comp. Matt. xxvii. 52.

[5] Valesius says that the Edessenes commenced their era with the [beginning of] the 117th Olympiad, the first year of the reign of Seleucus. The year 340 corresponds, therefore, with the fifteenth year of Tiberius.

THE TEACHING OF ADDÆUS THE APOSTLE.[1]

. . . .

Addæus[2] [said] to him: Because thou hast thus believed, I lay my hand upon thee in the name of Him in whom thou hast thus believed. And at the very moment that he laid his hand upon him he was healed of the plague of the disease which he had for a long time.[3] And Abgar was astonished and marvelled, because, like as he had heard about Jesus, how He wrought and healed, so Addæus also, without any medicine whatever, was healing in the name of Jesus. And Abdu also, son of Abdu, had the gout in his feet; and he also presented his feet to him, and he laid his hand upon them, and healed him, and he had the gout no more. And in all the city also he wrought great cures, and showed forth wonderful mighty-works in it.

Abgar said to him: Now that every man knoweth that by the power of Jesus Christ thou doest these miracles, and lo! we are astonished at thy deeds, I therefore entreat of thee to relate to us the story about the coming of Christ, in what manner it was, and about His glorious power, and about the miracles which we have heard that He did, which thou hast thyself seen, together with thy fellow-disciples.

Addæus said: I will not hold my peace from declaring this; since for this very purpose was I sent hither, that I might speak to and teach every one who is willing to believe, even as thou. Assemble me to-morrow all the city, and I will sow in it the word of life by the preaching which I will address to you —about the coming of Christ, in what manner it was; and about Him that sent Him, why and how He sent Him; and

---

[1] This fragment, extending to the lacuna on p. 14, is contained in the MS. No. 14,654, at fol. 33. It consists of one leaf only, and is part of a volume of fragments, of which the age is certainly not later than the beginning of the fifth century.

[2] [See note 1 on p. 10.]

[3] Moses Chor. says that he had been suffering seven years from a disease caught in Persia.

about His power and His wonderful works; and about the glorious mysteries of His coming, which He spake of in the world; and about the unerring truth[1] of His preaching; and how and for what cause He abased Himself, and humbled His exalted Godhead by the manhood which He took, and was crucified, and descended to the place of the dead, and broke through the enclosure[2] which had never been broken through [before], and gave life to the dead by being slain Himself, and descended alone, and ascended with many to His glorious Father, with whom He had been from eternity in one exalted Godhead.

And Abgar commanded them to give to Addæus silver and gold. Addæus said to him: How can we receive that which is not ours? For, lo! that which was ours have we forsaken, as we were commanded by our Lord [to do]; because without purses and without scrips, bearing the cross upon our shoulders, were we commanded to preach His gospel in the whole creation, of whose crucifixion, which was for our sakes, for the redemption of all men, the whole creation was sensible and suffered pain.

And he related before Abgar the king, and before his princes and his nobles, and before Augustin, Abgar's mother, and before Shalmath,[3] the daughter of Meherdath,[4] Abgar's wife,[5] the signs of our Lord, and His wonders, and the glorious mighty-works which He did, and His divine exploits, and His ascension to His Father; and how they had received power and authority at the same time that He was received up—by which same power it was that he had healed Abgar,

[1] "The certitude."—C.

[2] Eph. ii. 14.

[3] The vowels supplied in this word are conjectural, as is the case with most of the proper names in these Documents. Perhaps the name of this person is to be read Shalamtho, as there is a Σαλαμψιώ, the wife of Phasaëlus, mentioned in Jos. Antiq. b. xviii. c. v.

[4] Who this was, does not appear. He may have been some connection of Meherdates king of the Parthians, of whom Tacitus, Ann. xii. 12, speaks as having been entertained at Edessa by Abgar.

[5] According to Moses Chor. b. ii. ch. xxxv., the first, or chief, wife of Abgar was Helena.

and Abdu son of Abdu, the second person[1] of his kingdom; and how He informed them that He would reveal Himself at the end of the ages[2] and at the consummation of all created things; [he told them] also [of] the resuscitation and resurrection which is to come for all men, and the separation which will be made between the sheep and the goats, and between the faithful and those who believe not.

And he said to them: Because the gate of life is strait and the way of truth narrow, therefore are the believers of the truth few, and through unbelief is Satan's gratification. Therefore are the liars many who lead astray those that see. [Liars they are:] for, were it not that there is a good end awaiting believing men, our Lord would not have descended from heaven, and come to be born, and to [endure] the suffering of death. Yet He did come, and us did He send[3] .

. . . .
of the faith which we preach, that God was crucified for[4] all men.

And, if there be those who are not willing[4] to agree with these our words, let them draw near to us and disclose to us what is in their mind, that, like as in the case of a disease, we may apply to their thoughts healing medicine for the cure of their ailments. For, though ye were not present at the time of Christ's suffering, yet from the sun which was darkened, and which ye saw, learn ye and understand concerning the great convulsion[5] which took place at that time, when He

---

[1] Probably one of the second *rank*. Tacitus, *Ann.* vi. 31, 32, mentions a man named Abdus, perhaps the same as this one, as possessing great authority in the Parthian kingdom.

[2] [Or "times."]

[3] The remainder of "*The Teaching of Addæus*" is taken from another MS. of the Nitrian collection in the Brit. Mus., Cod. Add. 14,644. It is one of those which were procured in the year of the Greeks 1243 (A.D. 931) by the abbot Moses during his visit to Bagdad. It appears to be of the sixth century.

[4] Both "for" and "willing" are conjectural, the MS. being damaged. —Wright.

[5] [Possibly "earthquake," for which sense see Mich., p. 161; and so on p. 17.]

was crucified whose gospel has winged its way through all
the earth by the signs, which His disciples [my] fellows do in
all the earth: yea, those who were Hebrews, and knew only
the language of the Hebrews, in which they were born, lo!
at this day are speaking in all languages, in order that those
who are afar off may hear and believe, even as those who are
near. For He it is that confounded the tongues of the
presumptuous in this region who were before us; and He
it is that teaches at this day the faith of truth and verity
by us, humble and despicable [1] men from Galilee of Palestine. For I also whom ye see am from Paneas,[2] from the
place where the river Jordan issues forth, and I was chosen,
together with my fellows, to be a preacher.

. . . .

For, according as my Lord commanded me, lo! I preach
and publish the gospel, and lo! His money do I cast upon
the table before you, and the seed of His word do I sow in
the ears of all men; and such as are willing to receive it,
theirs is the good recompense of the confession [of Christ];
but those who are not persuaded [to accept it], the dust of
my feet do I shake off against them, as He commanded me.

Repent therefore, my beloved, of evil ways and of abominable deeds, and turn yourselves towards Him with a good
and honest will, as He hath turned Himself towards you
with the favour of His rich mercies; and be ye not as the
generations of former times that have passed away, which,
because they hardened their heart against the fear of God,
received punishment openly, that they themselves might be
chastised, and that those who come after them may tremble
and be afraid. For the purpose of our Lord's coming into the
world assuredly was,[3] that He might teach us and show us that
at the consummation of the creation there will be a resuscitation of all men, and that at that time their course of conduct will be portrayed in their persons, and their bodies will

---

[1] [Properly "miserable." Compare Rom. vii. 24; 1 Cor. xv. 19.]
[2] [Otherwise Cæsarea Paneas, or C. Philippi: now Banias.]
[3] [Cureton: "the whole object of our Lord's coming into the world
was." But ܓܠܡܐ is = *omnino*.]

be [so many] volumes for the writings of justice; nor will any one be there who is unacquainted with books, because every one will read that which is written in His own book.[1]

. . . .

Ye that have eyes, forasmuch as ye do not perceive, are yourselves also become like those who see not and hear not; and in vain do your ineffectual voices strain themselves to deaf[2] ears. Whilst *they* are not to be blamed for not hearing, because they are by[3] nature deaf and dumb, yet the blame which is justly incurred falls upon you,[4] because ye are not willing to perceive—not even that which ye see. For the dark cloud of error which overspreads your minds suffers you not to obtain the heavenly light, which is the understanding of knowledge.[5]

Flee, then, from things made and created, as I said to you, which are only called gods in name, whilst they are not gods in their nature; and draw near to this [Being], who in His nature is God from everlasting and from eternity, and is not something made, like your idols, nor is He a creature and a work of art, like those images in which ye glory. Because, although this[6] [Being] put on a body, [yet] is He God with His Father. For the works of creation, which trembled when He was slain and were dismayed at His suffering of death,—these bear witness that He is Himself God the Creator. For it was not on account of a man that the earth trembled,[7] but on account of Him who established the earth upon the waters; nor was it on account of a man that the sun grew dark in the heavens,

---

[1] A few lines are wanting here in the MS.

[2] The greater part of the word rendered "deaf" is conjectural.—WRIGHT. [The "your" looks as if it were impersonal: "it is useless for *any one* to talk to the deaf."]

[3] [" By " (ܒ) is not in the printed text.]

[4] [Lit. "the blame in which justice is involved (prop., buried) is yours."]

[5] [Comp. Prov. xix. 25.]   [6] " This " is doubtful.—WRIGHT.

[7] I have very little doubt that we should substitute ܐܪܥܐ ܙܥܬ [the earth trembled] for ܙܥܘ ܐܪܥܐ [who is from the earth].—WRIGHT.

but on account of Him who made the great lights; nor was it for a man that the just and righteous were restored to life again, but for Him who had granted power over death from the beginning; nor was it for a man that the veil of the temple of the Jews was rent from the top to the bottom, but for Him who said to them, "Lo, your house is left desolate." For, lo! unless those who crucified Him had known that He was the Son of God, they would not have had to proclaim [1] the desolation [2] of their city, nor would they have brought down Woe! upon themselves.[3] For, even if they had wished to make light of this confession,[4] the fearful convulsions which took place at that time would not have suffered them to do so. For lo! some even of the children of the crucifiers are become at this day preachers and evangelists, along with my fellow-apostles, in all the land of Palestine, and among the Samaritans, and in all the country of the Philistines. The idols also of paganism are despised, and the cross of Christ is honoured, and [all] nations and creatures confess God who became man.

If, therefore, while Jesus our Lord was on earth ye would have believed in Him that He is the Son of God, and before ye had heard the word of His preaching would have confessed Him that He is God; now that He is ascended to His Father, and ye have seen the signs and the wonders which are done in His name, and have heard with your own ears the word of His gospel, let no one of you doubt in

---

[1] [Lit. "have proclaimed."]

[2] [Cureton renders: "They would not have proclaimed the *desolation* of their city, nor would they have divulged the *affliction* of their soul in crying Woe!" Dr. Wright pronounces the two words whose equivalents are given in italics to be very doubtful. Dr. Payne Smith, instead of the latter of the two (ܐܠܨܐ), conjectures (ܐܘ ܕܢܒܣܪܘܢ). This conjecture has been adopted. "Brought down" (ܘܡܦܠܝܢ) is lit. "caused to drop."]

[3] The ancient Syriac Gospel, Luke xxiii. 48, gives: "And all those who were assembled there, and saw that which was done, were smiting on their breast, and saying, Woe to us! what is this? Woe to us for our sins!"

[4] [*i.e.* Christianity.]

his mind—so that the promise of His blessing which He sent to you may be fulfilled[1] towards you: Blessed are ye that have believed in me, not having seen me; and, because ye have so believed in me, the town[2] in which ye dwell shall be blessed, and the enemy shall not prevail against it for ever.[3] Turn not away, therefore, from His faith: for, lo! ye have heard and seen what things bear witness to His faith— [showing] that He is the adorable Son, and is the glorious God, and is the victorious King, and is the mighty Power; and through faith in Him a man is able to acquire the eyes of a true mind,[4] and to understand that, whosoever worshippeth creatures, the wrath of justice will overtake him.

[1] [Or "confirmed."]

[2] [Perhaps "town" will not seem too insignificant a word if it be taken in its original sense of a fortified place, which the Syriac term also denotes. It seemed desirable to distinguish, if possible, the two words which have been rendered respectively "city" and "town" in these pages. The only exception made is in a single passage where *Rome* is spoken of.]

[3] These words are not in the letter of Christ to Abgar. They must therefore be, either a message brought by Addæus himself, or, much more probably, a later interpolation: earlier, however, than Ephraem Syrus, who alludes to them in his *Testament*. This notion of the immunity of the city of Edessa is referred to by several Syriac writers. Nor was it confined to the East: it obtained in very early times in our own country, where the letter of our Lord to Abgar was regarded as a charm. In a very ancient service-book of the Saxon times, preserved in the British Museum, the letter follows the Lord's Prayer and the Apostles' Creed; and an appended description of the virtues of the epistle closes with these words, according to the Latin version of Rufinus: "*Si quis hanc epistolam secum habuerit, securus ambulet* [ambulabit?] *in pace.*" Jeremiah Jones, writing of the last century, says: "The common people in England have had it [the letter] in their houses in many places in a frame with a picture before it; and they generally, with much honesty and devotion, regard it as the word of God and the genuine epistle of Christ." Even now a similar practice is believed to linger in some districts. The story of Abgar is told in an Anglo-Saxon poem, published in *Abgarus-Legenden paa Old-Engelsk* by G. Stephens, Copenhagen, 1853. [It consists of 204 lines, is a tolerably close rendering of Eusebius, and is ascribed by Stephens to Aelfric, archbishop of York from 1023 to 1052.]

[4] See Eph. i. 18.

For [in] everything which we speak before you, according as we have received of the gift of our Lord, [so] speak we and teach and declare [it], that ye may secure[1] your salvation and not destroy[2] your spirits through the error of paganism: because the heavenly light has arisen on the creation, and He it is who chose the fathers of former times, and the righteous men, and the prophets, and spake with them in the revelation of the Holy Spirit.[3] For He is Himself the God of the Jews who crucified Him; and to Him it is that the erring pagans offer worship, even while they know it not: because there is no other God in heaven and on earth; and lo! confession ascendeth up to Him from the four quarters of the creation. Lo! therefore, your ears have heard that which was not heard by you [before]; and lo! further, your eyes have seen that which was never seen by you [before].

Be not, therefore, gainsayers of that which ye have seen and heard. Put away from you the rebellious mind of your fathers, and free yourselves from the yoke of sin, which hath dominion over you in libations and in sacrifices [offered] before carved images; and be ye concerned for your endangered[4] salvation, and for the unavailing support on which ye lean;[5] and get you a new mind, that worships the Maker and not the things which are made—[a mind] in which is portrayed the image of verity and of truth, of the Father, and of the Son, and of the Holy Spirit; believing and being baptized in the triple and glorious names. For this is our teaching and our preaching. For the belief of the truth of

---

[1] [Lit. "obtain."] [2] [Or "lose."] [3] [Lit. "Spirit of holiness."]

[4] [Prop. "lost," or "being lost," "perishing."]

[5] [Lit. "support of your head."] The word rendered "support" is not in the dictionaries, but its derivation and form are known. Mar Jacob, *infra*, has a similar expression: "A resting-place for the head, etc." [where, however, his word is derived from a root meaning to "prop up" (ܣܡܟ), whereas the root of our word denotes to "bend itself," "bow down" (ܟܦ), and is often used of the declining day (as Luke xxiv. 29). It is used of the bending of the head in John xix. 30. The actual *leaning* of the head for support is not expressed in the verb, but would naturally be inferred from it].

Christ does not consist of many things.[1] And those of you as are willing to be obedient to Christ are aware that I have many times repeated my words before you, in order that ye might learn and understand what ye hear.

And we ourselves shall rejoice in this, like the husbandman who rejoices in the field which is blessed; God also will be glorified by your repentance towards Him. While ye are saved hereby, we also, who give you this counsel, shall not be despoiled of the blessed reward of this [work]. And, because I am assured that ye are a land blessed according to the will of the Lord Christ, therefore, instead of the dust of our feet which we were commanded to shake off against the town that would not receive our words, lo! I have shaken off to-day at the door of your ears the sayings of my lips, in which are portrayed the coming of Christ which has [already] been, and also that which is [yet] to be; and the resurrection, and the resuscitation of all men, and the separation which is to be made between the faithful and the unbelieving; and the sore punishment which is reserved for those who know not God, and the blessed promise of future joy which they shall receive who have believed in Christ and worshipped Him and His exalted Father, and have confessed Him and His divine Spirit.[2]

And now it is meet for us that I conclude my present discourse; and let those who have accepted the word of Christ remain with us, and those also who are willing to join with us in prayer; and afterwards let them go to their homes.

And Addæus the apostle was rejoiced to see that a great number of the population of the city stayed with him; and they were [but] few who did not remain at that time, while even those few not many days after accepted his words and believed in the gospel set forth in[3] the preaching of Christ.

---

[1] [Lit. "the truth of Christ is not believed in many things."]

[2] [Lit. "the Spirit of His Godhead" = His Spirit of Godhead = His divine Spirit.]

[3] [Lit. "the gospel of."]

And when Addæus the apostle had spoken these things before all the town of Edessa, and King Abgar saw that all the city rejoiced in his teaching, men and women alike, and [heard them] saying to him, "True and faithful is Christ who sent thee to us"—he himself also rejoiced greatly at this, giving praise to God; because, like as he had heard from Hanan,[1] his Tabularius, about Christ, so had he seen the wonderful mighty-works which Addæus the apostle did in the name of Christ.

And Abgar the king also said to him: According as I sent [word] to Christ in my letter to Him, and according as He also sent [word] to me, [so] have I also received from thine own self this day; [and] so will I believe all the days of my life, and in the selfsame things will I continue and make my boast, because I know also that there is no other power in whose name these signs and wonders are done but the power of Christ whom thou preachest in verity and in truth. And henceforth Him will I worship—I and my son Maanu,[2] and Augustin,[3] and Shalmath the queen. And now, wherever thou desirest, build a church, a place of meeting for those who have believed and shall believe in thy words; and, according to the command given thee by thy Lord, minister thou at the [proper] seasons with confidence; to those also who shall be [associated] with thee as teachers of this gospel I am prepared to give large donations, in order that they may not have any other work beside the ministry; and whatsoever is required by thee for the expenses of the building I myself will give thee without any restriction,[4] whilst thy word shall be authoritative and sovereign in this town; moreover, without [the intervention of] any other person do thou come into my presence as one in authority, into the palace of my royal majesty.

[1] See p. 7.
[2] Abgar had two sons of this name. This is probably the elder, who succeeded his father at Edessa, and reigned seven years. Bayer makes him the fifteenth king of Edessa.
[3] Abgar's mother: see p. 13.
[4] [Lit. "reckoning."]

And when Abgar was gone down to his royal palace he rejoiced, he and his princes with him, Abdu son of Abdu, and Garmai, and Shemashgram,[1] and Abubai, and Meherdath,[2] together with the others their companions, at all that their eyes had seen and their ears also had heard; and in the gladness of their heart they too began to praise God for having turned their mind towards Him, renouncing the paganism in which they had lived,[3] and confessing the gospel of Christ. And when Addæus had built a church they proceeded to offer in it vows and oblations, they and the people of the city; and there they continued to present their praises all the days of their life.

And Avida and Barcalba,[4] who were chief men and rulers, and wore the royal headband,[5] drew near to Addæus, and asked him about the matter of Christ, [requesting] that he would tell them how He, though He was God, appeared to

---

[1] The vowels in this name are supplied from the treatise of Bardesan. Whiston, from the Armenian form, writes the name Samsagram. He was sent, together with Hanan and Maryhab, as envoy to Marinus. See Mos. Chor. B. ii. c. 30.

[2] See Tac. *Ann.* xii. 12.

[3] [Lit. "stood."]

[4] The son of Zati (see p. 29).

[5] [Or " the headbands of the kings." Nothing appears to be known of the derivation of the word ܣܢܘܐܪ̈ܐ, which does not occur in the ordinary lexicons. Dr. Payne Smith has favoured the translator with the following note: "ܣܢܘܐܪ̈ܐ is evidently some kind of ornament. In Ephs. ii. 379 (in the form ܣܢܘܐܪ̈ܐ) it is an ornament worn by young people. B.A. [Bar Alii *Lex. Syro-Arab.*] and K. [Georgii Karmsedinoyo *Lex.*] render it (in the form ܣܢܘܐܪ̈ܐ) مدور جارة, which may mean 'a circlet of jewels.'" Cureton says: "These headbands of the king, or diadems, seem to have been made of silk or muslin scarves, like the turbans of orientals at the present day, interwoven with gold, and with figures and devices upon them, as was the case with that worn by Sharbil. See *Acts of Sharbil, sub init.*" The art. *Diadema* in Dr. W. Smith's *Antiqq.* seems to furnish a good idea of what is intended. The ornament was probably *white;* and this has caused our expression to be sometimes confounded with the similar ܣܕܘܢܐ ܚܘܪܐ. See *Teaching of Simon Cephas*, init.]

them as a man: And how, said they, were ye able to look upon Him? And he proceeded to satisfy them all about this, about all that their eyes had seen and about whatsoever their ears had heard from him. Moreover, everything that the prophets had spoken concerning Him he repeated before them, and they received his words gladly and with faith, and there was not a man that withstood him; for the glorious deeds which he did suffered not any man to withstand him.

Shavida, moreover, and Ebednebu, chiefs of the priests of this town, together with Piroz[1] and Dilsu their companions, when they had seen the signs which he did, ran and threw down the altars on which they were accustomed to sacrifice before Nebu and Bel,[2] their gods, except the great altar which was in the middle of the town; and they cried out and said: Verily this is the disciple of that eminent and glorious Master, concerning whom we have heard all that He did in the country of Palestine. And all those who believed in Christ did Addæus receive, and baptized them in the name of the Father, and of the Son, and of the Holy Spirit. And those who used to worship stones and stocks sat at his feet, recovered from the madness[3] of paganism wherewith they had been afflicted. Jews also, traders in fine raiment,[4] who were familiar with the law and the prophets—they too were persuaded, and became disciples, and confessed Christ that He is the Son of the living God.

But neither did King Abgar nor yet the Apostle Addæus compel any man by force to believe in Christ, because without the force of man the force of the signs compelled many to believe in Him. And with affection did they receive His doctrine—[even] all this country of Mesopotamia, and all the regions round about it.

[1] The same name as Berosus, who is so called in the modern Persian.

[2] These were the chief gods of Edessa, the former representing the sun, and the latter the moon.

[3] [The reference seems to be to Mark v. 15.]

[4] The " soft [clothing] " of Matt. xi. 8, where [the Peshito and] the " Ancient Recension " have the same word as appears here. Cureton renders it "silk," but remarks: "It would appear to be cotton or muslin, *lana xylina*, not *bombycina*."

Aggæus, moreover, who[1] made the silks[2] and headbands of the king, and Palut, and Barshelama, and Barsamya, together with the others their companions, clave to Addæus the apostle; and he received them, and associated them with him in the ministry, their business being to read in the Old Testament and the New,[3] and in the prophets, and in the Acts of the Apostles, [and] to meditate upon them daily; strictly charging them to let their bodies be pure and their persons holy, as is becoming in men who stand before the altar of God. "And be ye," said he, "far removed from false swearing and from wicked homicide, and from dishonest testimony, which is connected with adultery; and from magic arts, for which there is no mercy, and from soothsaying, and divination, and fortune-tellers; and from fate and nativities, of which the deluded Chaldeans make their boast; and from the stars, and the signs of the Zodiac, in which the foolish put their trust. And put far from you unjust partiality, and bribes, and presents, through which the innocent are pronounced guilty. And along with this ministry, to which ye have been called, see that ye have no other work besides: for the Lord is the work of your ministry all the days of your life. And be ye diligent to give the seal of baptism.

---

[1] [The text has not ܘ, but it is best to supply it.]

[2] [Cureton gives "chains," which in his notes he changes to "silks," or "muslins," adopting, with C., the reading ܣܪ̈ܝܐ instead of the ܩܠܝܕ̈ܐ of the printed text. Mos. Chor. calls Aggæus "un fabricant de coiffures de *soie*," according to the translation of Florival; or "quendam *serici* opificem," according to Whiston. It may be added that the word ܣܪ̈ܝܐ is doubtless the same as our "silk," which is only a form of *Sericum*, an adjective from *Seres*, the people whose country was the native home of the silk-worm.]

[3] These terms could only have been used here in the sense of the Law of Moses and the Gospel. If by the Acts of the Apostles is meant the work of Luke, this passage seems to show that the compiler of this account of Addæus wrote some years subsequently to the events which he relates, or that it has been added by a later interpolator. For at the earlier period of Addæus' ministry no other part of the New Testament was written than the Hebrew Gospel of Matthew, which is probably the Gospel here meant.

And be not fond of the gains of this world. And hear ye a cause with justice and with truth. And be ye not a stumbling-block to the blind, lest through you should be blasphemed the name of Him who opened [the eyes of] the blind, according as we have seen. Let all, therefore, who see you perceive that ye yourselves are in harmony with whatsoever ye preach and teach."

And they ministered with him in the church which Addæus had built at the word and command of Abgar the king, being furnished with supplies by the king and by his nobles, partly for the house of God, and partly for the supply of the poor. Moreover, much people day by day assembled and came to the prayers of the service, and to [the reading of] the Old Testament, and the New of the Diatessaron.[1] They also believed in the restoration of the dead, and buried their departed in the hope of resuscitation [to life]. The festivals of the church they also observed in their seasons, and were assiduous every day in the vigils of the church. And they made visits of almsgiving, to the sick and to those that were whole, according to the instruction of Addæus to them. In the environs, too, of the city churches were built, and many received from him ordination to the priesthood.[2] So that even people of the East, in the guise of merchants, passed over into the territory of the Romans, that they might see the signs which Addæus did. And such as became disciples received from him ordination to the priesthood, and in their own country of the Assyrians they instructed the people of their nation, and erected houses of prayer there in secret, by reason of the danger [which beset them] from those who worshipped fire and paid reverence to water.[3]

---

[1] Or "Ditornon." The reading of the MS. is not clear. It seems that it ought to be *Diatessaron* [the two words would differ but slightly in the mode of writing], which Tatian the Syrian [Assyrian] compiled from the four Gospels about the middle of the second century. This was in general use at Edessa up to the fourth century, and Ephraem Syrus wrote a commentary on it. If this be so, we have here a later interpolation.

[2] [Lit. "the hand of priesthood:" and so *passim*.]

[3] Strabo, *de Persis*, b. xv. [ch. iii.]: "They sacrifice to fire and to water"

Moreover, Narses, the king of the Assyrians, when he heard of those same things which Addæus the apostle had done, sent [a message] to Abgar the king: Either despatch to me the man who doeth these signs before thee, that I may see him and hear his word, or send me [an account of] all that thou hast seen him do in thy own town. And Abgar wrote to Narses,[1] and related to him the whole story of the deeds of Addæus from the beginning to the end; and he left nothing which he did not write to him. And, when Narses heard those things which were written to him, he was astonished and amazed.

Abgar the king, moreover, because he was not able to pass over into the territory of the Romans,[2] and go to Palestine and slay the Jews for having crucified Christ, wrote a letter and sent it to Tiberius Cæsar,[3] writing in it thus:—

King Abgar to our Lord Tiberius Cæsar: Although I know that nothing is hidden from thy Majesty, I write to inform thy dread and mighty Sovereignty that the Jews who are under thy dominion and dwell in the country of Palestine have assembled themselves together and crucified Christ, without any fault [worthy] of death [in Him], after He had done before them signs and wonders, and had shown them powerful mighty-works, so that He even raised the dead to life for them; and at the time that they crucified Him the sun became darkened and the earth also quaked, and all created things trembled and quaked, and, as if of themselves, at this deed the whole creation and the inhabitants of the creation shrank away. And now thy Majesty knoweth what it is meet for thee to command concerning the people of the Jews who have done these things.

And Tiberius Cæsar wrote and sent to King Abgar; and thus did he write to him:—

The letter of thy Fidelity towards me I have received, and it hath been read before me. Concerning what the Jews

---

[1] See his letter in Mos. Chor., *infra*.

[2] Dio Cassius, liv. 8: "Augustus fixed as the boundaries of the empire of the Romans the Tigris and Euphrates."

[3] See it also, with some variations, in Mos. Chor., *infra*.

have dared to do in the matter of the cross, Pilate[1] the governor also has written and informed Aulbinus[2] my proconsul concerning these selfsame things of which thou hast written to me. But, because a war with the people of Spain,[3] who have rebelled against me, is on foot at this time, on this account I have not been able to avenge this matter; but I am prepared, when I shall have leisure, to issue a command according to law against the Jews, who act not according to law. And on this account, as regards Pilate also, who was appointed by me governor there—I have sent another in his stead, and dismissed him in disgrace, because he departed from the law,[4] and did the will of the Jews, and for the gratification of the Jews crucified Christ, who, according to what I hear concerning Him, instead of [suffering] the cross of death, deserved to be honoured and worshipped[5] by them:

[1] It was Pilate's duty, as governor of Judea, to send an account to the Roman Government of what had occurred in respect to Jesus; and his having done so is mentioned by Justin Martyr, Tertullian, and several other writers.

[2] The word is evidently misspelt. The name intended may have been confounded with that of the Albinus who was made governor of Judea at a later period by Nero, A.D. 62. The same person is referred to, in the *Exit of Mary, infra*: "Sabinus, the governor who had been appointed by the Emperor Tiberius; and even as far as the river Euphrates the governor Sabinus had authority." The person meant can only be Vitellius, who was then governor of Syria, who removed Pilate from the administration of Judea, sending Marcellus in his stead, and ordered him to appear before Tiberius at Rome. The emperor died before he reached Rome.

[3] No mention is made by historians of any war with Spain. But about this time Vitellius, mentioned in the preceding note, was mixed up with the wars of the Parthians and Hiberians; and, as Hiberi is a name common to Spaniards as well as Hiberians, the apparent error may have arisen in translating the letter out of Latin into Syriac.

[4] Baronius says Pilate violated the law by crucifying our Lord so soon after sentence had been passed, whereas a delay of ten days was required by a law passed in the reign of Tiberius.

[5] Tiberius is said by Tertullian (*Apol.* 5) to have referred to the senate the question of admitting Christ among the gods. This has been interpolated into the epistle of Tiberius to Abgar as given in Moses Chor., B. ii. c. 33. He also adds another letter from Abgar in reply to this.

and more especially because with their own eyes they saw everything that He did. Yet thou, in accordance with thy fidelity towards me, and the faithful covenant [entered into by] thyself and by thy fathers, hast done well in writing to me thus.

And Abgar the king received Aristides, who had been sent by Tiberius Cæsar to him; and in reply he sent him [back] with presents of honour suitable for him who had sent him to him. And from Edessa he went to Thicuntha,[1] where Claudius, the second from the emperor, was; and from thence, again, he went to Artica,[2] where Tiberius Cæsar was: Caius, moreover, was guarding the regions round about Cæsar. And Aristides himself also related before Tiberius concerning the mighty-works which Addæus had done before Abgar the king. And when he had leisure from the war he sent and put to death some of the chief men of the Jews who were in Palestine. And, when Abgar the king heard of this, he rejoiced greatly that the Jews had received punishment, as it was right.

And some years after Addæus the apostle had built the church in Edessa, and had furnished it with everything that was suitable for it, and had made disciples of a great number of the population of the city, he further built churches in the villages[3] also—[both] those which were at a distance and those which were near, and finished and adorned them, and appointed in them deacons and elders, and instructed in

---

[1] This word has been so much distorted and disfigured by the transcribers, that I am unable to recognise what is the place intended.—Cureton.

[2] This word may be read *Ortyka*, and may be intended for *Ortygia* near Syracuse, which was not far from the island of Capreæ, where Tiberius then resided, seldom leaving it to go farther than to the neighbouring coast of Campania.

[3] [Lit. "the *other* villages." So, in several passages of these Documents, "the rest of the other ——." The habit of including two or more distinguished notions under a class to which only one of them belongs was not unknown among classical writers also: as when, *e.g.*, Thucydides speaks of the Peloponnesian war as the most remarkable of all the wars that *preceded* it. Milton's imitation, "Fairest of all her daughters, Eve," is well known.]

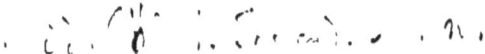

them those who should read the Scriptures, and taught the ordinances and[1] the ministry without and within.

After all these things he fell ill of the sickness of which he departed from this world. And he called for Aggæus before the whole assembly of the church, and bade him draw near, and made him Guide and Ruler[2] in his stead. And Palut,[3] who was a deacon, he made elder; and Abshelama, who was a scribe, he made deacon. And, the nobles and chief men being assembled, and standing near him—Barcalba son of Zati,[4] and Maryhab[5] son of Barshemash, and Senac[6] son of Avida, and Piroz son of Patric,[7] together with the rest of their companions—Addæus the apostle said to them:—

"Ye know and are witness, all of you who hear me, that, [according to] all that I have preached to you and taught you and ye have heard from me, even so have I behaved myself in the midst of you, and ye have seen [it] in deeds also: because our Lord thus charged us, that, whatsoever we preach in words before the people, we should practise it in deeds before all men. And, according to the ordinances and

---

[1] The ☉ (and) seems to have been altered into ? (of).—WRIGHT. [Perhaps "of" is the better reading.]

[2] It is plain from the context here, as well as wherever it occurs in these early Syriac Documents, that this title [or that of Guide alone] is precisely the same as that of Bishop, although the Greek word ἐπίσκοπος had not yet obtained in the East. The first mention we find of the title *Bishop* [in these pages] is in the *Acts of Sharbil* about A.D. 105–112, where Barsamya is called "the Bishop of the Christians," although he is more generally designated as here. It is also found in the *Teaching of Simon Cephas, sub fin.*, which seems to have been written early in the second century or at the end of the first. The passage in the *Teaching of Addæus*, p. 35, where it occurs, was interpolated at a much later period.

[3] Perhaps Φιλώτας.

[4] Perhaps the same as Izates: see Jos. *Antiq.* xx. ii. 1, 4; Tac. *Ann.* xii. 14.

[5] This seems to be the person spoken of by Moses Chor., B. ii. c. 30, under the name "Mar-Ihap, prince d'Aghtznik," as one of the envoys sent by Abgar to Marinus.

[6] Tacitus writes this name Sinnaces: see *Ann.* vi. 31, 32.

[7] Patricius.

laws which were appointed by the disciples in Jerusalem,[1] and by which my fellow-apostles also guided their conduct, so also [do] ye—turn not aside from them, nor diminish aught from them: even as I also am guided by them amongst you, and have not turned aside from them to the right hand or to the left, lest I should become estranged from the promised salvation which is reserved for such as are guided by them.

"Give[2] heed, therefore, to this ministry which ye hold, and with fear and trembling continue in it, and minister every day. Minister not in it with neglectful habits, but with the discreetness of faith; and let not the praises of Christ cease out of your mouth, nor let weariness of prayer at the [stated] times come upon you. Give heed to the verity which ye hold, and to the teaching of the truth which ye have received, and to the inheritance of salvation which I commit to you: because before the tribunal of Christ will ye have to give an account of it, when He maketh reckoning with the shepherds and overseers, and when He taketh His money from the traders with the addition of the gains. For He is the Son of a King, and goeth to receive a kingdom and return; and He will come and make a resuscitation [to life] for all men, and then will He sit upon the throne of His righteousness, and judge the dead and the living, as He said to us.

"Let not the secret eye of your minds be closed by pride, lest your stumbling-blocks be many in the way in which there are no stumbling-blocks, but a hateful[3] wandering in its paths. Seek ye those that are lost, and direct those that go astray, and rejoice in those that are found; bind up the bruised, and watch over the fatlings: because at your hands will the sheep of Christ be required. Look ye not for the honour that passeth away: for the shepherd that looketh to receive honour from his flock—sadly, sadly stands his

---

[1] These are given at pp. 38 sqq.

[2] Quoted in the *Epistle of Addæus, infra*.

[3] [Probably "wicked," the meaning being that all such wandering is wilful. Cureton makes "hateful" the *predicate:* "error is abominable in its paths."]

flock with respect to him. Let your concern be great for the young lambs, whose angels behold the face of the Father who is unseen. And be ye not stones of stumbling before the blind, but clearers of the way and the paths in a rugged country, among the Jews the crucifiers, and the deluded pagans: for with these two parties have ye to fight, in order that ye may show the truth of the faith which ye hold; and, though ye be silent, your modest and decorous appearance will fight for you against those who hate truth and love falsehood.

"Buffet not the poor in the presence of the rich: for scourge grievous enough for them is their poverty.

"Be not beguiled by the hateful devices of Satan, lest ye be stripped naked of the faith which ye have put on."[1] . .

. . . .

"And with the Jews, the crucifiers, we will have no fellowship. And this inheritance which we have received from thee we will not let go, but in that will we depart out of this world; and on the day of our Lord, before the judgment-seat of His righteousness, there will He restore to us this inheritance, even as thou hast told us."

And, when these things had been spoken, Abgar the king rose up, he and his chief men and his nobles, and he went to his palace, all of them being distressed for him because he was dying. And he sent to him noble and excellent apparel, that he might be buried in it. And, when Addæus saw it, he sent [word] to him, [saying]: In my lifetime I have not taken anything from thee, nor will I now at my death take anything from thee, nor will I frustrate the word of Christ which He spake to us: Accept not anything from any man, and possess not anything in this world.[2]

And three days more after these things had been spoken by Addæus the apostle, and he had heard and received the testimony concerning the teaching set forth in their preaching

---

[1] One leaf apparently is lost from the MS. in this place. [What follows appears to be part of the reply of those addressed—their "testimony concerning the teaching set forth in their preaching."]

[2] The reference seems to be to Matt. x. 7–10.

from those engaged with him in the ministry, in the presence of all the nobles he departed out of this world. And that day was the fifth of the week, and the fourteenth of the month Iyar.¹ And the whole city was in great mourning and bitter anguish for him. Nor was it the Christians only that were distressed for him, but the Jews also, and the pagans, who were in this same town. But Abgar the king was distressed for him more than any one, he and the princes of his kingdom. And in the sadness of his soul he despised and laid aside the magnificence of his kingly state on that day, and with tears mingled with moans he bewailed him with all men. And all the people of the city that saw him were amazed [to witness] how greatly he suffered on his account. And with great and surpassing pomp he bore [him to his grave], and buried him like one of the princes when he dies; and he laid him in a grand sepulchre adorned with sculpture wrought by the fingers—that in which were laid those of the house of Ariu, the ancestors of Abgar the king: there he laid him sorrowfully, with sadness and great distress. And all the people of the church went there from time to time and prayed fervently; and they kept up the remembrance of his departure from year to year, according to the command and direction which had been received by them from Addæus the apostle,² and according to the word of Aggæus, who himself became Guide and Ruler, and the successor of his seat after him, by the ordination to the priesthood which he had received from him in the presence of all men.

He too, with the same ordination which he had received from him, made Priests and Guides in the whole of this country of Mesopotamia. For they also, in like manner as Addæus the apostle, held fast his word, and listened to and received [it], as good and faithful successors of the apostle of the adorable Christ. But silver and gold he took not

¹ [Nearly answering to] May. The death of Addæus occurred before that of Abgar, which took place A.D. 45. It would appear, therefore, that his ministry at Edessa lasted about ten or eleven years.
² Compare the *Teaching of the Apostles*, Ordinance xviii. p. 41.

from any man, nor did the gifts of the princes come near him : for, instead of [receiving] gold and silver, he [himself] enriched the church of Christ with the souls of believers.

Moreover, [as regards] the entire state[1] of the men and the women, they were chaste and circumspect, and holy and pure : for they lived like anchorites[2] and chastely, without spot—in [their] circumspect watchfulness touching the ministry, in their sympathy[3] toward the poor, in their visitations to the sick : for their footsteps were fraught with praise from those who saw [them], and their conduct was arrayed in commendation from strangers—so that even the priests of the house of[4] Nebu and Bel divided the honour with them at all times, by reason of their dignified aspect, their truthful words, their frankness of speech arising from their noble nature, which was neither subservient through covetousness nor in bondage under [the fear of] blame. For there was no one who saw them that did not run to meet them, that he might salute them respectfully, because the very sight of them shed peace upon the beholders: for just like a net[5] were their words of gentleness spread over the contumacious, and they entered within the fold of truth and verity. For there was no man who saw them that was ashamed of them, because they did nothing that was not accordant with rectitude and propriety. And in consequence of these things their bearing was fearless as they published their teaching to all men. For, whatsoever they said to others and enjoined on them, they themselves exhibited in practice in their own persons ; and the hearers, who saw that their actions went along with their words, without much persuasion became their disciples, and confessed the King Christ, praising God for having turned them towards Him.

---

[1] This seems to apply to those who especially belonged to the ministry of the church. [This is the only passage in the Documents in which women are spoken of as connected with the ministry.]

[2] [The reference is only to their purity of life. It is not implied that they lived in seclusion.]

[3] [Lit. "their burden-bearing."]   [4] [Or "belonging to."]

[5] An allusion to Matt. iv. 19 : "I will make you fishers of men."

And some years after the death of Abgar the king, there arose one of his contumacious[1] sons, who was not favourable to peace; and he sent [word] to Aggæus, as he was sitting in the church: Make me a headband of gold, such as thou usedst to make for my fathers in former times. Aggæus sent [word] to him: I will not give up the ministry of Christ, which was committed to me by the disciple of Christ, and make a headband of wickedness. And, when he saw that he did not comply, he sent and brake his legs[2] as he was sitting in the church expounding. And as he was dying he adjured Palut and Abshelama: In this house, for whose truth's sake, lo! I am dying, lay me and bury me. And, even as he had adjured [them], so did they lay him—inside the middle door of the church, between the men and the women. And there was great and bitter mourning in all the church, and in all the city—over and above the anguish and the mourning which there had been within [the church], such as had been the mourning when Addæus the apostle himself died.

[And,[3] in consequence of his dying suddenly and quickly at the breaking of his legs, he was not able to lay [his] hand upon Palut. [So] Palut went to Antioch, and received ordination to the priesthood from Serapion bishop of An-

---

[1] [*i.e.* refusing to accept Christianity: as a few lines before.] The person referred to would seem to be the second of the two sons of Abgar called Maanu, who succeeded his brother Maanu, and reigned fourteen years—from A.D. 52 to A.D. 65, according to Dionysius as cited by Assemani.

[2] This ignominious mode of execution, which was employed in the case of the two thieves at Calvary, seems to have been of Roman origin. The object of the king in putting Aggæus to this kind of death was, probably, to degrade and disgrace him.

[3] This paragraph is a barefaced interpolation made by some ignorant person much later (who is also responsible for the additions to the *Martyrdom of Sharbil*, and to that of Barsamya). For this Palut was made *Elder* by Addæus himself, at the time that Aggæus was appointed *Bishop*, or *Guide and Ruler*. This took place even before the death of Abgar, who died A.D. 45; whereas Serapion did not become bishop of Antioch till the beginning of the third century, if, as is here stated, he was consecrated by Zephyrinus, who did not become Pope till A.D. 201.

tioch; by which Serapion himself also ordination had been received from Zephyrinus bishop of the city of Rome, in the succession of the ordination to the priesthood from Simon Cephas, who had received [it] from our Lord, and was bishop there in Rome twenty-five years in the days of the Cæsar who reigned there thirteen years.]

And, according to the custom which exists in the kingdom of Abgar the king, and in all kingdoms, that whatsoever the king commands and whatsoever is spoken in his presence is committed to writing and deposited among the records, so also did Labubna,[1] son of Senac, son of Ebedshaddai, the king's scribe, write these things also relating to Addæus the apostle from the beginning to the end, whilst Hanan also the Tabularius, a sharir of the kings, set-to his hand in witness, and deposited [the writing] among the records of the kings, where the ordinances and laws are deposited, and where [the contracts of] the buyers and sellers are kept with care, without any negligence whatever.

[Here] endeth the teaching of Addæus the apostle, which he proclaimed in Edessa, the faithful city of Abgar, the faithful king.

THE TEACHING OF THE APOSTLES.[2]

At what time Christ was taken up to His Father; and how the apostles received the gift of the Spirit; and the

---

[1] Moses Chor., ii. 36, calls him, in the translation of Le Vaillant de Florival, "Ghéroupna, fils de l'écrivain Apchatar;" in that of Whiston, "Lerubnas, Apsadari scribæ filius." Apchatar of the first, and Apsadar of the second, translator are evidently corruptions in the Armenian from the Adbshaddai (= Ebedshaddai) of the Syriac. Dr. Alishan, in a letter to Dr. Cureton from the Armenian Convent of St. Lazarus, Venice, says he has found an Armenian MS., of probably the twelfth century, which he believes to be a translation of the present Syriac original. It is a history of Abgar and Thaddæus, written by Ghérubnia with the assistance of Ananias (= Hanan), confidant (= sharir) of King Abgar.

[2] This work is taken, and printed verbatim, from the same MS. as

Ordinances and Laws of the church; and whither each one of the apostles went; and from whence the countries in the territory of the Romans received the ordination to the priesthood.

In the year three hundred and[1] thirty-nine of the kingdom of the Greeks, in the month Heziran,[2] on the fourth[3] day of the same, which is the first day of the week, and the end of Pentecost[4]—on the selfsame day came the disciples from Nazareth of Galilee, where the conception of our Lord was announced, to the mount which is called that of the Place of Olives,[5] our Lord being with them, but not being visible to them. And at the time of early dawn our Lord lifted up His hands, and laid them upon the heads of the eleven disciples, and gave to them the gift of the priesthood. And suddenly a bright cloud received Him. And they saw Him as He was going up to heaven. And He sat down on the right hand of His Father. And they praised God because they saw His ascension according as He had told them; and they rejoiced because they had received the Right Hand conferring on them the priesthood of the house of Moses and Aaron.

And from thence they went up [to the city], and[6]

the preceding, Cod. Add. 14,644, fol. 10. That MS., however, has been carefully compared with another in the Brit. Mus. in which it is found, Cod. Add. 14,531, fol. 109; and with a third, in which the piece is quoted as *Canons of the Apostles*, Cod. Add. 14,173, fol. 37. In using the second, a comparison has also been made of De Lagarde's edition of it (Vienna, 1856). This treatise had also been published before in *Ebediesu Metropolitæ Sobæ et Armeniæ collectio canonum Synodicorum* by Cardinal Mai. It is also cited by Bar Hebræus in his *Nomocanon*, printed by Mai in the same volume. These three texts are referred to in the notes, as A. B. C. respectively.

[1] A. omits "three hundred and." They are supplied from B. The reading of C. is 342.

[2] [This month answers to Sivan, which began with the new moon of June.]

[3] C. reads "fourteenth."

[4] The day of Pentecost seems to be put for that of the Ascension.

[5] Syr. "Baith Zaithe." Comp. Luke xxiv. 50 sqq.

[6] Comp. Acts i. 12 sqq.

proceeded to an upper room—that in which our Lord had observed the passover with them, and the place where the inquiries had been made: Who it was that should betray our Lord to the crucifiers? There also were the inquiries [made]: How they should preach His gospel in the world? And, as within the upper room the mystery of the body and of the blood of our Lord began to prevail in the world, so also from thence did the teaching of His preaching begin to have authority in the world.

And, when the disciples were cast into this perplexity, how they should preach His gospel to [men of] strange tongues which were unknown to them, and were speaking thus to one another: Although we are confident that Christ will perform by our hands mighty works and miracles in the presence of strange peoples whose tongues we know not, and who themselves also are unversed in our tongue, [yet] who shall teach them and make them understand that it is by the name of Christ who was crucified that these mighty works and miracles are done?—while, I say, the disciples were occupied with these thoughts, Simon Cephas rose up, and said to them: My brethren, this matter, how we shall preach His gospel, pertaineth not to us, but to our Lord; for *He* knoweth how it is possible for us to preach His gospel in the world; and we rely on His care for us, which He promised us, saying: "When I am ascended to my Father I will send you the Spirit, the Paraclete, that *He* may teach you everything which it is meet for you to know, and to make known."

And, whilst Simon Cephas was saying these things to his fellow-apostles, and putting them in remembrance, a mysterious voice was heard by them, and a sweet odour, which was strange to the world, breathed upon them;[1] and tongues of fire, between the voice and the odour, came down from heaven[2] towards them, and alighted on every one of them and sat [upon him]; and, according to the tongue which every one of them had severally received, so did he prepare

---

[1] The reading of B. and C.: A. reads "answered them."
[2] B. reads "suddenly."

himself to go to the country in which that tongue was spoken and heard.

And, by the same gift of the Spirit which was given to them on that day, they appointed Ordinances and Laws—such as were in accordance with the gospel of their preaching, and with the true and faithful doctrine of their teaching:—

1. The apostles therefore appointed: Pray ye towards the east:[1] because, "as the lightning which lighteneth from the east and is seen even to the west, so shall the coming of the Son of man be"[2]—[which was said] that by this we might know and understand that He will appear from the east suddenly.[3]

2. The apostles further appointed: On the first [day] of the week let there be service, and the reading of the Holy Scriptures, and the oblation:[4] because on the first day of the week our Lord rose from the place of the dead, and on the first day of the week He arose upon the world, and on the first day of the week He ascended up to heaven, and on the first day of the week He will appear at last with the angels of heaven.[5]

3. The apostles further appointed: On the fourth[6] day of the week let there be service: because on that [day] our Lord made the disclosure to them about His trial[7] and His suffering, and His crucifixion, and His death, and His resurrection; and the disciples were on account of this in sorrow.[8]

4. The apostles further appointed: On the eve [of the Sabbath],[9] at the ninth hour, let there be service: because

---

[1] On praying towards the east, comp. *Apost. Constitutions*, ii. 57, vii. 44; and Tertullian, *Apol.* 16. [*A. C.* ii. 57, contains an interesting account of the conduct of public worship. It may be consulted in connection with Ordinances 2, 8, and 10, also.]

[2] Matt. xxiv. 27.

[3] B. and C. read "at the last." Ebediesu has "from heaven."

[4] [*i.e.* the Eucharist.]   [5] C. reads "His holy angels."

[6] For Ords. 3 and 4, see *Ap. Const.* v. 13-15.

[7] B. reads "His manifestation."

[8] The reading of C., [which is preferable to that of A.: "were in this sorrow."]

[9] [Lit. "the evening," but used in particular of the evening of the

that which had been spoken on the fourth day of the week about the suffering of the Saviour was brought to pass on the eve [of the Sabbath], the worlds and [all] creatures trembling, and the luminaries in the heavens being darkened.

5. The apostles further appointed: Let there be elders and deacons, like the Levites;[1] and subdeacons,[2] like those who carried the vessels of the court of the sanctuary of the Lord; and an overseer,[3] who shall likewise be the Guide of all the people,[4] like Aaron, the head and chief of all the priests and Levites of the whole city.[5]

6. The apostles further appointed: Celebrate the day of the epiphany[6] of our Saviour, which is the chief of the festivals of the church, on the sixth day of the latter Canun,[7] in the long number of the Greeks.[8]

7. The apostles further appointed: Forty[9] days before the day of the passion of our Saviour fast ye, and then celebrate the day of the passion, and the day of the resurrection: because our Lord Himself also, the Lord of the festival,

---

sixth day of the week, the eve of the seventh: the evening being regarded, as in Gen. i. 5, as the first part of the day. Similarly, παρασκευή, which the Peshito translates by our word, is used in the Gospels for the sixth day, with a prospective reference to the seventh.]

[1] See *Ap. Const.* ii. 25.

[2] [Comp. *Eccl. Canons*, No. 43. The Gr. ὑποδιάκονοι is here used, though for "deacon" the usual Syriac word is employed, meaning "minister" or "servant." From Riddle, *Christian Antiqq.*, p. 301, with whom Neander agrees, it would seem that subdeacons were first appointed at the end of the third century or the beginning of the fourth.]

[3] ܣܟܘܦܐ, equivalent, not to ἐπίσκοπος, but to σκοπός = *watchman*, as in Ezek. xxxiii. 7.

[4] For this B. reads "world."   [5] B. has "camp."

[6] See *Ap. Const.* v. 13, [where Christmas, of which no mention is made in these Ordinances, is called "the first of all," the Epiphany being ranked next to it.]

[7] [January: the Jewish Tebeth. "The former Canun" is December, *i.e.* Chisleu.]

[8] [The era of the Seleucidæ, 311 A.C., appears to be referred to. In this new names were given to certain months, and Canun was one of them. See note on the Calendar at the end.]

[9] See *Ap. Const.* v. 13–15; [also *Eccl. Can.* No. 69.]

fasted forty days; and Moses and Elijah, who were endued with this mystery, likewise each fasted forty days, and then were glorified.

8. The apostles further appointed: At the conclusion of all the Scriptures [that are read] let the Gospel be read, as being the seal[1] of all the Scriptures; and let the people listen to it standing upon their feet: because it is the Gospel of the redemption of all men.

9. The apostles further appointed: At the completion of fifty[2] days after His resurrection make ye a commemoration of His ascension to His glorious Father.

10. The apostles [further] appointed: That, beside the Old Testament, and the Prophets, and the Gospel, and the Acts [descriptive] of their exploits, nothing should be read on the pulpit in the church.[3]

11. The apostles further appointed: Whosoever is unacquainted with the faith of the church and the ordinances and laws which are appointed in it, let him not be a guide and ruler; and whosoever is acquainted with them and departs from them, let him not minister again: because, not being true in his ministry, he has lied.

12. The apostles further appointed: Whosoever sweareth, or[4] lieth, or beareth false witness, or hath recourse to magicians and soothsayers and Chaldeans, and putteth confidence in fates and nativities, which they hold fast who know not God,—let him also, as a man that knoweth not God, be dismissed from the ministry, and not minister [again].

13. The apostles further appointed: If there be any man that is divided [in mind] touching the ministry, and who follows it not with a stedfast will,[5] let not this man minister

---

[1] [Properly "the sealer:" for, although the word is not found in the lexicons, its formation shows that it denotes an agent. The meaning seems to be, that the Gospel gives completeness and validity to the Scriptures.]

[2] C. reads "forty."

[3] [See *Ap. Const.* ii. 57; *Teaching of Simon Cephas, ad fin.; Eccl. Can.* Nos. 60, 85.]

[4] B. and C., as well as Ebediesu, read "and."

[5] [Lit., "it is not certain (or firm) to him."]

again: because the Lord of the ministry is not served by him with a stedfast will; and he deceiveth man [only], and not God, " before whom crafty devices avail not." [1]

14. The apostles further appointed: Whosoever lendeth and receiveth usury,[2] and is occupied in merchandise and covetousness, let not this man minister again, nor continue in the ministry.

15. The apostles further appointed: That whosoever loveth the Jews,[3] like Iscariot, who was their friend, or the pagans, who worship creatures instead of the Creator,—should not enter in amongst them and minister; and moreover, that if he be [already] amongst them, they should not suffer him [to remain], but that he should be separated from amongst them, and not minister with them again.

16. The apostles further appointed: That, if any one from the Jews or from the pagans come and join himself with them, and if after he has joined himself with them he turn and go back again to the side on which he stood [before], and if he again return and come to them a second time,—he should not be received again; but that, according to the side on which he was before, so those who know him should look upon him.

17. The apostles further appointed: That it should not be permitted to the Guide to transact the matters which pertain to the church apart from those who minister with him; but that he should issue commands with the counsel of them all, and that that [only] should be done which all of them should concur in and not disapprove.[4]

18. The apostles further appointed: Whenever any shall depart out of this world with a good testimony to the faith

---

[1] The exact words of the Peshito of 1 Sam. ii. 3. The E. V., following the K'ri ולו, instead of the ולא of the text, renders "and by Him actions are weighed." [The Peshito translator may have confounded the Heb. verb תכן, which appears not to exist in Aramæan, with his own verb תקן (ܬܩܢ), through the similarity in sound of the gutturals כ and ק.]

[2] [See *Eccl. Canons*, No. 44.]

[3] [Comp. *Eccl. Canons*, Nos. 65, 70, 71.]

[4] [See *Eccl. Canons*, No. 35.]

of Christ, and with affliction [borne] for His name's sake, make ye a commemoration of them on the day on which they were put to death.[1]

19. The apostles further appointed: In the service of the church repeat ye the praises of David day by day: because of this [text]: "I will bless the Lord at all times, and at all times His praises [shall be] in my mouth;"[2] and [this]: "By day and by night will I meditate and speak, and cause my voice to be heard before Thee."

20. The apostles further appointed: If any divest themselves of mammon and run not after the gain of money, let these men be chosen and admitted to the ministry of the altar.

21. The apostles further appointed: Let any priest who accidentally puts [another] in bonds[3] contrary to justice receive the punishment that is right; and let him that has been bound receive the bonds as if he had been equitably bound.

22. The apostles further appointed: If it be seen that those who are accustomed to hear causes show partiality, and pronounce the innocent guilty and the guilty innocent, let them never again hear another cause: [thus] receiving the rebuke of their partiality, as it is fit.[4]

23. The apostles further ordained: Let not those that are high-minded and lifted up with the arrogance of boasting be admitted to the ministry: because of this [text]: "That which is exalted among men is abominable before God;" and because concerning them it is said: "I will return a recompense upon those that vaunt themselves."

24. The apostles further appointed: Let there be a Ruler over the elders who are in the villages, and let him be recog-

---

[1] See the letter of the Church of Smyrna on the martyrdom of Polycarp, and Euseb. *Hist. Eccl.* iv. 15.

[2] Ps. xxxiv. 1.

[3] [The particip. ܣܐܒ, though usually pass., may, like some other participles Peil, be taken actively, as appears from a passage quoted by Dr. R. Payne Smith, *Thes. Syr. s.v.* This would seem to be the only possible way of taking it here.]

[4] Comp. *Ap. Const.* ii. 45 sqq.

nised as head of them all, at whose hand all of them shall be required: for Samuel also thus made visits [of inspection] from place to place and ruled.

25. The apostles further appointed: That those kings who shall hereafter believe in Christ should be permitted to go up and stand before the altar along with the Guides of the church: because David also, and those who were like him, went up and stood before the altar.

26. The apostles further appointed: Let no man dare to do anything by the authority of the priesthood which is not in accordance with justice and equity, but [let everything be done] in accordance with justice, and free from the blame of partiality.

27. The apostles further appointed: Let the bread of the oblation be placed upon the altar on the day on which it is baked, and not some days after—a thing which is not permitted.

All these things did the apostles appoint, not for themselves, but for those who should come after them—for they were apprehensive that in time to come wolves would put on sheep's clothing: since for themselves the Spirit, the Paraclete, which was in them, was sufficient [to secure] that, even as He had appointed these laws by their hands, [so] He would guide them [to act] lawfully. For they, who had received from our Lord power and authority, had no need that laws should be appointed for them by others. For Paul also, and Timothy,[1] while they were going from place to place in the country of Syria and Cilicia, committed these same Commands and Laws of the apostles and elders to those who were under the hand of the apostles, for the churches of the countries in which they were preaching and publishing the gospel.

The disciples, moreover, after they had appointed these Ordinances and Laws, ceased not from the preaching of the gospel, or from the wonderful mighty-works which our Lord did by their hands. For much people was gathered about them every day, who believed in Christ; and they

---

[1] Acts xvi. 4; comp. ch. xv.

came to them from other cities, and heard their words and received them. Nicodemus also, and Gamaliel, chiefs of the synagogue of the Jews, used to come to the apostles in secret, agreeing with their teaching. Judas, moreover, and Levi, and Peri, and Joseph, and Justus, sons of Hananias, and Caïaphas [1] and Alexander the priests—they too used to come to the apostles by night, confessing Christ that He is the Son of God; but they were afraid of the people of their own nation, so that they did not disclose their mind toward the disciples.

And the apostles received them affectionately, saying to them: Do not, by reason of the shame and fear of men, forfeit your salvation before God, nor have the blood of Christ required of you; even as your fathers, who took it upon them: for it is not acceptable before God, that, while ye are [of one mind] with His worshippers, ye should go and associate with the murderers of His adorable Son. How do ye expect that your faith should be accepted with those that are true, whilst ye are [found] with those that are false? But it becomes you, as men who believe in Christ, to confess openly this faith which we preach.

And, when they heard these things from the Disciples, those sons of the priests, all of them alike, cried out before the whole company of the apostles: We confess and believe in Christ who was crucified, and we confess that He is from everlasting the Son of God; and those who dared to crucify Him do we renounce. For even the priests of the people in secret confess Christ; but, for the sake of the headship among the people which they love, they are not willing to confess [Him] openly; and they have forgotten that which is written: "Of knowledge is He the Lord, and before Him avail not crafty devices."

And, when their fathers heard these things from their sons, they became exceedingly hostile to them: not indeed

---

[1] The belief was common among the Jacobites that Caïaphas, whose full name was Joseph Caïaphas, was the same person as the historian Josephus, and that he was converted to Christianity. See Assem. *Bibl. Orient.* vol. ii. p. 165.

because they had believed in Christ, but because they had declared and spoken openly of the mind of their fathers before the sons of their people.

But those who believed clave to the disciples, and departed not from them, because they saw that, whatsoever they taught the multitude, they themselves carried into practice before all men; and, when affliction and persecution arose against the disciples, they rejoiced to be afflicted with them, and received with gladness stripes and imprisonment for the confession of their faith in Christ; and all the days of their life they preached Christ before the Jews and the Samaritans.

And after the death of the apostles there were Guides and Rulers[1] in the churches; and, whatsoever the apostles had committed to them and they had received from them, they continued to teach to the multitude through the whole space of their lives. They too, again, at their deaths committed and delivered to their disciples after them whatsoever they had received from the apostles; also what James had written from Jerusalem, and Simon from the city of Rome, and John from Ephesus, and Mark from Alexandria the Great, and Andrew from Phrygia, and Luke from Macedonia, and Judas Thomas from India:[2] that the epistles of an apostle[3] might be received and read in the churches that were in every place, just as the achievements of their Acts, which Luke wrote, are read; that hereby the apostles might be known, and the prophets, and the Old Testament and the New;[4]

---

[1] This would seem to have been written anterior to the time when the title of Bishop, as specially appropriated to those who succeeded to the apostolic office, had generally obtained in the East.

[2] [For writings ascribed to Andrew and Thomas, see vol. xvi. of the *Ante-Nicene Christian Library*.] There is no mention here of the epistles of Paul. They may not at this early period have been collected and become generally known in the East. The Epistle of Jude is also omitted here, but it was never received into the Syriac canon: see De Wette, *Einl.* 6th ed. p. 342. [Comp. *Eccl. Canons*, No. 85.]

[3] [So the printed text. But "the apostles" seems to be meant.]

[4] It is plain from this that the epistles were not at that time considered part of what was called the New Testament, nor the prophets of the Old. [See note on p. 24.]

that [it might be seen that] one truth was proclaimed in them all: that one Spirit spake in them all, from one God whom they had all worshipped and had all preached. And the [various] countries received their teaching. Everything, therefore, which had been spoken by our Lord by means of the apostles, and which the apostles had delivered to their disciples, was believed and received in every country, by the operation[1] of our Lord, who said to them: "I am with you, even until the world shall end;" the Guides disputing with the Jews from the books of the prophets, and contending also against the deluded pagans with the terrible mighty-works which they did in the name of Christ. For all the peoples, even those that dwell in other countries, quietly and silently received[2] the gospel of Christ; and those who became confessors cried out under their persecution: This our persecution to-day shall plead[3] on our behalf, [that we be not punished] for having been formerly persecutors [ourselves]. For there were some of them against whom death by the sword was ordered; and there were some of them from whom they took away whatsoever they possessed, and let them go. And the more affliction arose against them, the richer and larger did their congregations become; and with gladness in their hearts did they receive death of every kind. And by ordination to the priesthood, which the apostles themselves had received from our Lord, did their gospel wing its way rapidly into the four quarters of the world. And by mutual visitation they ministered to one another.

Jerusalem received the ordination to the priesthood, as did all the country of Palestine, and the parts occupied by the Samaritans, and the parts occupied by the Philistines, and the country of the Arabians, and of Phœnicia, and the people of Cæsarea, from James, who was ruler and guide in the church of the apostles which was built in Zion.

Alexandria the Great, and Thebais, and the whole of Inner

---

[1] [Lit. "nod," or "bidding," or "impulse."]
[2] [Lit. "were quiet and silent at."]
[3] [Lit. "be an advocate."]

Egypt, and all the country of Pelusium,[1] and [the country extending] as far as the borders of the Indians, received the apostles' ordination to the priesthood from Mark the evangelist, who was ruler and guide there in the church which he had built, [in which] he also ministered.

India,[2] and all the countries belonging to it and round about it, even to the farthest sea, received the apostles' ordination to the priesthood from Judas Thomas, who was guide and ruler in the church which he had built there, [in which] he also ministered there.

Antioch, and Syria, and Cilicia, and Galatia, even to Pontus, received the apostles' ordination to the priesthood from Simon Cephas, who himself laid the foundation of the church there,[3] and was priest and ministered there up to the time when he went up from thence to Rome on account of Simon the sorcerer, who was deluding the people of Rome with his sorceries.

The city of Rome, and all Italy, and Spain, and Britain, and Gaul, together with all the rest of the countries round about them, received the apostles' ordination to the priesthood from Simon Cephas, who went up from Antioch; and he was ruler and guide there, in the church which he had built there, and in the places round about it.

Ephesus, and Thessalonica, and all Asia, and all the country of the Corinthians, and of all Achaia and the parts round about it, received the apostles' ordination to the priesthood from John the evangelist, who had leaned upon the bosom of our Lord; who himself built a church there, and ministered in his office of guide which [he held] there.

Nicæa, and Nicomedia, and all the country of Bithynia, and of Inner Galatia,[4] and of the regions round about it,

---

[1] C. reads "Pentapolis."

[2] A. has "the Indians;" C. "the Ethiopians."

[3] C. adds, "and built a church at Antioch."

[4] [The reading of C. The MS. A. gives what Cureton transcribes as Gothia, which is almost the same as the word rendered "Inner." Possibly this explains the origin of the reading of A. "Galatia" was perhaps accidentally omitted.]

received the apostles' ordination to the priesthood from Andrew, the brother of Simon Cephas, who was himself guide and ruler in the church which he had built there, and was priest and ministered there.

Byzantium, and all the country of Thrace, and of the parts about it as far as the great river,[1] the boundary which separates from the barbarians, received the apostles' ordination to the priesthood from Luke the apostle, who himself built a church there, and ministered there in his office of ruler and guide which [he held] there.

Edessa, and all the countries round about it which were on all sides of it, and Zoba,[2] and Arabia, and all the north, and the regions round about it, and the south, and all the region on the borders of Mesopotamia, received the apostles' ordination to the priesthood from Addæus the apostle, one of the seventy-two apostles,[3] who himself made disciples there, and built a church there, and was priest and ministered there in his office of guide which [he held] there.

The whole of Persia, of the Assyrians, and of the Armenians, and of the Medians, and of the countries round about Babylon, the Huzites and the Gelæ, as far as the borders of the Indians, and as far as the land[4] of Gog and Magog, and moreover all the countries on all sides, received the apostles' ordination to the priesthood from Aggæus, a maker of silks,[5] the disciple of Addæus the apostle.

The other remaining companions of the apostles, moreover, went to the distant countries of the barbarians; and they made disciples from place to place and passed on; and there they ministered by their preaching; and there occurred their departure out of this world, their disciples after them going on [with the work] down to the present day, nor was any change or addition made by them in their preaching.

---

[1] C. has "the Danube." [2] Or "Soba," the same as Nisibis.

[3] The number seventy-two may have arisen from the supposition, mentioned in the *Recognitions* and in the *Apostolical Constitutions*, that our Lord chose them in imitation of the seventy-two elders appointed by Moses.

[4] [Or "place."] [5] See note on p. 24.

Luke, moreover, the evangelist had such diligence that he wrote the exploits of the Acts of the Apostles, and the ordinances and laws of the ministry of their priesthood, and whither each one of them went. By his diligence, I say, did Luke write these things, and more than these; and he placed them in the hand of Priscus[1] and Aquilus, his disciples; and they accompanied him up to the day of his death, just as Timothy and Erastus of Lystra, and Menaus,[2] the first disciples of the apostles, accompanied Paul until he was taken up to the city of Rome because he had withstood Tertullus the orator.

And Nero Cæsar despatched with the sword Simon Cephas in the city of Rome.[3]

---

[4]THE TEACHING OF SIMON CEPHAS[5] IN THE CITY OF ROME.

In the third[6] year of Claudius Cæsar, Simon Cephas departed from Antioch to go to Rome. And as he passed on he preached in the [various] countries the word of our Lord. And, when he had nearly arrived there,[7] many had heard [of it] and went out to meet him, and the whole church received him with great joy. And some of the princes of the city, wearers of the imperial headbands,[8]

---

[1] B. reads "Priscilla," C. "Priscillas." Prisca and Priscilla are the forms in which the name occurs in the New Testament.

[2] Probably the same as Manaen, mentioned in Acts xiii. 1, as associated with Paul at Antioch.

[3] C. adds, "crucifying him on a cross." C. also adds, "Here endeth the treatise of Addæus the apostle."

[4] This is found in the same MS. as the preceding, quoted as A. There is also another copy of it in Cod. Add. 14,609, referred to here as B.

[5] B. reads "the Apostle Peter."

[6] The reading of the MS. is "thirtieth."

[7] From this place to "the light," p. 51, line 22, A. is lost, and the text has been supplied from B.

[8] The MS. gives, "clad in the white."

D

came to him, that they might see him and hear his word. And, when the whole city was gathered together about him, he stood up to speak to them, and to show them the preaching of his doctrine, of what sort it was. And he began to speak to them thus:—

Men, people of Rome, saints of all Italy, hear ye that which I say to you. This day I preach and proclaim Jesus the Son of God, who came down from heaven, and became man, and was with us as [one of] ourselves, and wrought marvellous mighty-works and signs and wonders before us, and before all the Jews that are in the land of Palestine. And you yourselves also heard of those things which He did: because they came to Him from other countries also, on account of the fame of His healing and the report of the marvellous help He gave;[1] and whosoever drew near to Him was healed by His word. And, inasmuch as He was God, at the same time that He healed He also forgave sins: for His healing, which was open to view, bore witness of His hidden forgiveness, that it was real and trustworthy. For this Jesus did the prophets announce in their mysterious sayings, as they were looking forward to see Him and to hear His word, [as] Him who was with His Father from eternity and from everlasting; God, who was hidden in the height, and appeared in the depth; the glorious Son, who was from His Progenitor, and is to be glorified, together with His Father, and His divine Spirit, and the terrible power of His dominion. And He was crucified of His own will by the hands of sinners, and was taken up to His Father, even as I and my companions saw. And He is about to come again, in His own glory and that of His holy angels, even as we heard Him say to us. For we cannot say anything which was not heard by us from Him, neither do we write in the book of His Gospel anything which He Himself did not say to us: because this word is spoken in order that the mouth of liars may be shut, in the day when men shall give an account of idle words at the place of judgment.

[1] [Lit. "His marvellous helps."]

Moreover, because we were catchers of fish, and not skilled in books, therefore did He also say to us: "I will send you the Spirit, the Paraclete, that He may teach you that which ye know not;" for it is by *His* gift that we speak those things which ye hear. And, further, by it we bring aid to the sick, and healing to the diseased: that by the hearing of His word and by the aid of His power ye may believe in Christ, that He is God, the Son of God; and may be delivered from the service of bondage, and may worship Him and His Father, and glorify His divine Spirit. For when we glorify the Father, we glorify the Son also with Him; and when we worship the Son, we worship the Father also with Him; and when we confess the Spirit, we confess the Father also and the Son: because in the name of the Father, and of the Son, and of the Spirit, were we commanded to baptize those who believe, that they may live for ever.

Flee therefore from the words of the wisdom of this world, in which there is no profit, and draw near to those which are true and faithful, and acceptable before God; whose reward also is laid up in store, and whose recompense standeth [sure]. Now, too,[1] the light has arisen on the creation, and the world has obtained the eyes of the mind, that every man may see and understand that it is not fit that creatures should be worshipped instead of the Creator, nor together with the Creator: because everything which is a creature is [formed to be] a worshipper of its Maker, and is not to be worshipped like its Creator. But this [Being] who came to us is God, the Son of God, in His own nature, notwithstanding that He mingled[2] His Godhead with our manhood, in order that He might renew our man-

---

[1] [The text A. is resumed after this word. The reading "and now that the light," etc., seems faulty. The ? (that) might easily have been occasioned by the ? of the word which it precedes.]

[2] The word so rendered is much effaced in B., but it seems to be ܡܟܣ, "humbled." [This, however, might require a further change of the text, such as Cureton suggests, so as to give the sense, "He humbled His Godhead *on account of* our manhood," unless we translate "*in* our

hood by the aid of His Godhead. And on this account it is right that we should worship Him, because He is to be worshipped together with His Father, and that we should not worship creatures, who were created for the worship of the Creator. For He is Himself the God of truth and verity; He is Himself from before [all] worlds and creatures; He is Himself the veritable Son, and the glorious fruit[1] which is from the exalted Father.

But ye see the wonderful works which accompany and follow these words. One would not credit it: the time lo! is short since He ascended to His Father, and see how His gospel has winged its flight through the whole creation—that thereby it may be known and believed that He Himself is the Creator of creatures, and that by His bidding creatures subsist. And, whereas ye saw the sun become darkened at His death, ye yourselves also are witnesses. The earth, moreover, quaked when He was slain, and the veil was rent at His death. And concerning these things the governor Pilate also was witness: for he himself sent and made them known to Cæsar, and these things, and more than these, were read before him, and before the princes of your city. And on this account Cæsar was angry against Pilate, because he had unjustly listened to the persuasion of the Jews; and for this reason he sent and took away from him the authority which he had given to him. And this same thing was published and known in all the dominion of the Romans. That, therefore, which Pilate saw and made known to Cæsar and to your honourable senate, the same do I preach and declare, as do also my fellow-apostles. And ye know that Pilate could not have written to the imperial government of that which did not take place and which he had not seen with his own eyes; but that which did take place and was actually done—this it was that he wrote and made known.

---

manhood"—neither of which renderings seems to give so good a sense as that in the text of A.] Respecting the word " mingled " (ܡܙܓ), which was supposed to countenance the Eutychian heresy, see Assemani, *Bibl. Orient.* vol. i. p. 81.

[1] [Or "offspring."]

Moreover, the watchers of the sepulchre also were witnesses of those things which took place there: they became as dead men; and, when those watchers were questioned before Pilate, they confessed before him how large a bribe the chief-priests of the Jews had given them, so that they might say that we His disciples had stolen the corpse of Christ. Lo! then, ye have heard many things; and moreover, if ye be not willing to be persuaded by those things which ye have heard, be at least persuaded by the mighty-works which ye see, which are done by His name.

Let not Simon the sorcerer delude you by semblances which are not realities, which he exhibits to you, as to men who have no understanding, who know not how to discern that which they see and hear. Send, therefore, and fetch him to where all your city is assembled together, and choose you some sign for us to do before you; and, whichever ye see do that same sign, it will be your part to believe in it.

And immediately they sent and fetched Simon the sorcerer; and the men who were adherents of his opinion said to him: As a man concerning whom we have confidence that there is power in thee to do anything whatsoever,[1] do thou some sign before us all, and let this Simon the Galilæan, who preaches Christ, see [it]. And, whilst they were thus speaking to him, there happened to be passing along a dead person, a son of one of those who were chiefs and men of note and renown among them. And all of them, as they were assembled together, said to him: Whichever of you shall restore to life this dead person, he is true, and to be believed in and received, and we will all follow him in whatsoever he saith to us. And they said to Simon the sorcerer: Because thou wast here before Simon the Galilæan, and we knew thee before him, exhibit thou first the power which accompanieth thee.

Then Simon reluctantly drew near to the dead person; and they set down the bier before him; and he looked to the right hand and to the left, and gazed up into heaven, saying

[1] From this place to "a gathering-place," p. 55, line 15, the text of A. is lost.

many words: some of them he uttered aloud, and some of them secretly and not aloud. And he delayed a long while, and nothing took place, and nothing was done, and the dead person was [still] lying upon his bier.

And forthwith Simon Cephas drew near boldly towards the dead man, and cried aloud before all the assembly which was standing there: In the name of Jesus Christ, whom the Jews crucified at Jerusalem, and whom we preach, rise up thence. And as soon as the word of Simon was spoken the dead man came to life and rose up from the bier.

And all the people saw [it] and marvelled; and they said to Simon: Christ, whom thou preachest, is true. And many cried out, and said: Let Simon the sorcerer and the deceiver of us all be stoned. But Simon, by reason that every one was running to see the dead man that was come to life, escaped from them from one street to another and from house to house, and fell not into their hands on that day.

But the whole city took hold of Simon Cephas, and they received him gladly and affectionately; and he ceased not from doing signs and wonders in the name of Christ; and many believed in him. Cuprinus,[1] moreover, the father of him that was restored to life, took Simon with him to his house, and entertained him in a suitable manner, while he and all his household believed in Christ, that He is the Son of the living God. And many of the Jews and of the pagans became disciples there. And, when there was great rejoicing at his teaching, he built churches there, in Rome and in the cities round about, and in all the villages of the people of Italy; and he served there [in] the rank of the Superintendence of Rulers twenty-five years.[2]

And after these years Nero Cæsar seized him and shut him up in prison. And he knew that he would crucify him;

---

[1] Perhaps Cyprianus, which is found written in Syriac in the same manner as the word here.

[2] This is the time usually allotted to Peter's episcopate at Rome, although it is certain that he did not constantly reside there during that period: we find him the year after at Jerusalem.

so he called Ansus,[1] the deacon, and made him bishop in his stead in Rome. And these things did Simon himself speak; and moreover also the rest, the other things which he had [in charge], he commanded Ansus to teach before the people, saying to him: Beside the New Testament and the Old let there not be read before the people[2] anything else,[3] [a thing] which is not right.

And, when Cæsar had commanded that Simon should be crucified with his head downwards, as he himself had requested of Cæsar, and that Paul's head should be taken off, there was great commotion among the people, and bitter distress in all the church, seeing that they were deprived of the sight of the apostles. And Isus the guide arose and took up their bodies by night, and buried them with great honour, and there came to be a gathering-place there for many.

And at that very time, as if by a righteous judgment, Nero abandoned his empire and fled, and there was a cessation for a little while from the persecution which Nero Cæsar had raised against them. And many years after the great coronation[4] of the apostles, who had departed out of the world, while ordination to the priesthood was proceeding both in all Rome and in all Italy, it happened then that there was a great famine in the city of Rome.[5]

Here endeth the teaching of Simon Cephas.

---

[1] B. has Lainus = *Linus*, the person undoubtedly meant. The error arose chiefly from the ܠ (L) being taken as the sign of the accusative case, [which may be omitted]. Below, the name appears as Isus, and in the *Acts of Barsamya*, p. 90, we have Anus.

[2] In canon x. (see next note) it is said "in the pulpit of the church;" and in the *Teaching of Addæus* it is said that "a large multitude of the people assembled for the reading of the Old Testament and the New." The inhibition seems, therefore, to refer only to public reading.

[3] This agrees with the tenth canon in the *Teaching of the Apostles*.

[4] That is, their martyrdom. But B. reads "labour."

[5] This abrupt termination seems to indicate that there was something more which followed. The famine referred to seems to be the same as that mentioned in the interpolated passage at the end of the *Acts of Sharbil*.

ACTS OF SHARBIL,[1] WHO WAS A PRIEST OF IDOLS, AND WAS CONVERTED TO THE CONFESSION OF CHRISTIANITY IN CHRIST.

In the fifteenth year of the Sovereign Ruler[2] Trajan Cæsar,[3] and in the third year of King Abgar the Seventh,[4] which is the year 416 of the kingdom of Alexander king of the Greeks, and in the priesthood of Sharbil and Barsamya,[5] Trajan Cæsar commanded the governors of the countries under his dominion that sacrifices and libations should be increased in all the cities of their administration, and that those who did not sacrifice should be seized and delivered over to stripes, and to [the tearing of] combs, and to bitter inflictions of all [kinds of] tortures, and should afterwards receive the punishment of the sword.

Now, when the command arrived at the town of Edessa of

---

[1] There are two MSS. from which this piece is taken. The first is Cod. Add. 14,644, fol. 72 vers. This, which is referred to as A., has been copied exactly, except that a few manifest errors have been corrected and some deficiencies supplied from the other. This latter, quoted as B., is Cod. Add. 14,645. It is some three or four centuries later than the first.—[The Latin *Acta*, to which the Greek ὑπομνήματα here employed corresponds, was used to denote the authorized records of judicial proceedings.] They were first taken down by shorthand-writers, called *notarii* (notaries), [*actuarii*,] or [at a later period] *exceptores*, by which name they are mentioned towards the end of this extract; the Greeks called them ταχυγράφοι. They were then arranged in proper order by persons called by the Greeks ὑπομνηματογράφοι, and by the Romans *Ab Actis*.—The use of ὑπομνήματα and other Greek words seems to show that these Acts were originally written in that language.

[2] [Αὐτοκράτωρ.]

[3] That is, A.D. 112. But the Greek era commences 311 or 312 B.C., and therefore A.G. 416 would answer to A.D. 105. There appears to be some error in the date.

[4] The king reigning in the fifteenth year of Trajan was Maanu Bar Ajazath, the seventh king of Edessa after Abgar the Black.

[5] It would thus appear that Paganism and Christianity were tolerated together in Edessa at this time, equal honour being attributed to the head of each religious party. Comp. *Teaching of Addæus*, p. 23: "Neither did King Abgar compel any man by force to believe in Christ."

the Parthians, there was a great festival, on the eighth of Nisan, on the third [day] of the week: the whole city was gathered together by the great altar[1] which was in the middle of the town, opposite the Record office,[2] all the gods having been brought together, and decorated, and sitting in honour, both Nebu and Bel together with their fellows. And all the priests were offering incense of spices and libations,[3] and an odour of sweetness was diffusing itself around, and sheep and oxen were being slaughtered, and the sound of the harp and the drum was heard in the whole town. And Sharbil was chief and ruler of all the priests; and he was honoured above all his fellows, and was clad in splendid and magnificent vestments; and a headband embossed with figures of gold was set upon his head; and at the bidding of his word everything that he ordered was done. And Abgar the king, son of the gods, was standing at the head of the people. And they obeyed Sharbil, because he drew nearer to all the gods than any of his fellows, and as being the one who [according to] that which he had heard from the gods returned an answer to every man.

And, while these things were being done by the command of the king, Barsamya, the bishop of the Christians, went up to Sharbil, he and Tiridath the elder and Shalula the deacon; and he said to Sharbil, the high-priest: The King Christ, to whom belong heaven and earth, will demand an account at thy hands of all these souls against whom thou art sinning, and whom thou art misleading, and turning away from the God of verity and of truth to idols [that are] made and deceitful, which are not able to do anything with their hands—moreover also thou hast no pity on thine own soul, which is destitute of the true life of God; and thou declarest to this people that the dumb idols talk with thee; and, as if thou wert listening to

---

[1] A little before the passage quoted in the last note it is said that this altar was left standing when the altars to Bel and Nebu were thrown down.
[2] Perhaps this is the same as the "Archives" mentioned p. 7.
[3] B. adds, "before the god Zeus."

something from them, thou puttest thine ear near to one and another of them, and sayest to this people: The god Nebu bade me say to you, "On account of your sacrifices and oblations I cause peace in this your country;" and: Bel saith, "I cause great plenty in your land;" and those who hear [this] from thee do not discern that thou art greatly deceiving them—because "they have a mouth and speak not, and they have eyes and see not with them;" it is ye who bear up them, and not they who bear up[1] you, as ye suppose; and it is ye who set tables before them, and not they who feed you. And now be persuaded by me touching that which I say to thee and advise thee. If thou be willing to hearken to me, abandon idols made [with hands], and worship God the Maker [of all things], and His Son Jesus Christ. Do not, because He put on a body and became man and was stretched out on the cross of death, be ashamed of Him and refuse to worship Him: for, all these things which He endured—it was for the salvation of men and for their deliverance [that He endured them]. For this [Being] who put on a body is God, the Son of God, Son of the essence of His Father, and Son of the nature of Him who begat Him: for He is the adorable brightness of His Godhead, and is the glorious manifestation of His majesty, and together with His Father He existed from eternity and from everlasting, His arm, and His right hand, and His power, and His wisdom, and His strength, and the living Spirit which is from Him, the Expiator and Sanctifier of all His worshippers. These [are the] things which Palut taught us, with whom thy venerable self[2] was acquainted; and thou knowest that Palut was the disciple of Addæus the apostle. Abgar the king also, who was older than this Abgar, who himself worshippeth idols as well as thou, he too believed in the King Christ, the

---

[1] B. adds here: "And in all these things thou hast forgotten God, the Maker of all men, and because of His long-suffering hast exalted thyself against His mercy, and hast not been willing to turn to Him, so that He might turn to thee and deliver thee from this error, in which thou standest."

[2] [Lit. "thy old age."]

Son of Him whom thou callest Lord of all the gods.[1] For it is forbidden to Christians to worship anything that is made, and is a creature, and in its nature is not God: even as ye worship idols made by men,[2] who themselves also are made and created. Be persuaded, therefore, by these things which I have said to thee, which things are the belief of the church: for I know that all this population are looking to thee, and I am well assured that, if thou be persuaded, many also will be persuaded with thee.[3]

Sharbil said to him: Very acceptable to me are these thy words which thou hast spoken before me; yea, exceedingly acceptable are they to me. But, as for me, I know that I am outcast from [4] all these things, and there is no longer any remedy for me. And, now that hope is cut off from me, why weariest thou thyself about a man dead and buried,[5] for whose death there is no hope of resuscitation? For I am slain by paganism, and am become a dead man, [the property] of the Evil One: in sacrifices and libations of imposture have I consumed all the days of my life.

And, when Barsamya the bishop heard these things,[6] he fell down before his feet, and said to him: There *is* hope for those who turn, and healing for those that are wounded. I myself will be surety to thee for the abundant mercies of the Son Christ: that He will pardon thee all the sins which thou hast committed against Him, in that thou hast worshipped and honoured His creatures instead of Himself. For that Gracious One, who extended Himself on the cross of death, will not withhold His grace from the souls that comply [with

---

[1] The Peshito, for Ζεύς in Acts xiv. 12, has "Lord of the gods."

[2] B. has "the work of men's hands."

[3] [B. makes a considerable addition here, which it is hardly necessary to quote, the words being in all probability only an interpolation. Cureton elsewhere remarks: "I have almost invariably found in these Syriac MSS. that the older are the shorter, and that subsequent editors or transcribers felt themselves at liberty to add [to] occasionally or paraphrase the earlier copies which they used"—a remark unhappily of very wide application in regard to early Christian literature.]

[4] [Or "destitute of."]   [5] [Lit. "a hidden dead man."]

[6] B. adds, "from Sharbil, his tears flowed and he wept."

His demands] and take refuge in His kindness which has been [displayed] towards us: like as He did towards the robber, [so] is He able to do to thee, and also to those who are like thee.

Sharbil said to him: Thou, like a skilful physician, who [himself] suffers pain from the pain of the afflicted, hast done well in that thou hast been concerned about me. But at present, because it is the festival to-day of this people, of every one [of them], I cannot go down with thee to-day to the church. Depart thou, and go down with honour; and to-morrow at night I will come down to thee: I too have henceforth renounced for myself the gods made [with hands], and I will confess the Lord Christ, the maker of all men.

And the next day Sharbil arose and went down to Barsamya by night, he and Babai his sister; and he was received by the whole church. And he said to them: Offer for me prayer and supplication, that Christ may forgive me all the sins that I have committed against Him in all this long course of years. And, because they were in dread of the persecutors, they arose and gave him the seal of salvation,[1] whilst he confessed the Father, and the Son, and the Holy Spirit.

And, when all the city had heard that he was gone down to the church, there began to be a consternation among the multitude; and they arose and went down to him, and saw him clad in the fashion of the Christians.[2] And he said to them: May the Son Christ forgive me all the sins that I have committed against you, and all [the instances in] which I made you think that the gods talked with me, whereas they did not talk; and, forasmuch as I have been to you a cause of abomination, may I now be to you a cause of good: in-

---

[1] B. adds, "of baptism, baptizing him." [The "seal" ($\sigma\varphi\rho\alpha\gamma\iota\varsigma$) is probably explained by such passages as Eph. iv. 30, that which bore the seal being regarded as the property of him whose seal it was. Thus Gregory Naz. (Orat. 40) speaks of baptism. See Riddle's *Christian Antiqq.* p. 484.]

[2] B. adds, "and he sat and listened to the Scriptures of the church, and the testimonies which are spoken in them, touching the birth and the passion and the resurrection and the ascension of Christ; and, when he saw those that came down to him—"

stead of worshipping, as formerly, idols made [with hands], may ye henceforth worship God the Maker [of all things]. And, when they had heard these things, there remained with him a great congregation of men and of women; and Labu also, and Hafsai, and Barcalba, and Avida, chief persons of the city. [And] they all said to Sharbil: Henceforth we also renounce that which thou hast renounced, and we confess the King Christ, whom thou hast confessed.

But Lysanias,[1] the judge of the country, when he heard [2] that Sharbil had done this,[3] sent by night [4] and carried him off from the church. And there went up with him many [of the] Christians. And he sat down, to hear him and to judge him, before the altar which is in the middle of the town, where he used to sacrifice to the gods. And he said to him: Wherefore hast thou renounced the gods, whom thou didst worship, and to whom thou didst sacrifice, and to whom thou wast made chief of the priests, and lo! dost to-day confess Christ, whom thou didst formerly deny? For see how those Christians, to whom thou art gone [over], renounce not that which they have held,[5] like as thou hast renounced that in which thou wast born. If thou art assured of [the existence of] the gods, how is it that thou hast renounced them this day? But, if on the contrary thou art not assured, as thou declarest concerning them, how is it that thou didst [once] sacrifice to them and worship them?

Sharbil said: When I was blinded in my mind, I worshipped that which I knew not; but to-day, inasmuch as I have obtained the clear eyes of the mind, it is henceforth impossible that I should stumble at carved stones, or that I should

---

[1] In B., in a passage added further on, he is styled "Lysinas," and in the *Martyrdom of Barsamya*, p. 81, "Lysinus" or "Lucinus." In the *Martyrologium Romanum* he is called "Lysias præses." Tillemont supposes him to be Lusius Quietus. But the time does not agree. The capture of Edessa under this man was in the nineteenth year of Trajan, four years later than the martyrdom.

[2] B. adds, "from the Sharirs of the city."

[3] B. has added several lines here.

[4] B. adds, "the Sharirs of the city."

[5] [Lit. "in which they stand."]

any longer be the cause of stumbling to others. For it is a great disgrace to him whose eyes are open, if he goes and falls into the pit of destruction.

The judge said: Because thou hast been priest of the venerable gods, and hast been partaker of the mystery of those whom the mighty emperors [1] worship, I will have patience with thee, in order that thou mayest be persuaded by me, and not turn away from the service of the gods; but, if on the contrary thou shalt not be persuaded by me, by those same gods whom thou hast renounced I swear that, even as on a man that is a murderer, so will I inflict tortures on thee, and will avenge on thee the wrong done to the gods, whom thou hast rebelled against and renounced, and also the insult which thou hast poured upon them; nor will I leave [untried] any kind of tortures which I will not inflict on thee; and, like as thine honour formerly was great, so will I make thine ignominy great this day.

Sharbil said: I too, on my part, am not content that thou shouldest look upon me as formerly, when I worshipped gods made [with hands]; but look thou upon me to-day and question me as a Christian man renouncing idols and confessing the King Christ.

The judge said: How is it that thou art not afraid of the emperors, nor moved to shame by those who are listening to thy trial, that thou sayest, "I am a Christian?" But promise that thou wilt sacrifice to the gods, according to thy former custom, so that thy honour may be great, as formerly —lest I make to tremble at thee all those who have believed like thyself.

Sharbil said: Of the King of kings I am afraid, but at [any] king of earth I tremble not, nor yet at thy threats towards me, which lo! thou utterest against the worshippers of Christ: whom I confessed yesterday, and lo! I am brought to trial for His sake to-day, like as He Himself was brought to trial for the sake of sinners like me.

The judge said: Although thou have no pity on thyself, still I will have pity on thee, and refrain from cutting off

---

[1] [Lit. "kings:" and so throughout.]

those hands of thine with which thou hast placed incense before the gods, and from stopping with thy blood those ears of thine which have heard their mysteries, and thy tongue which has interpreted and explained to us their secret things. Of those [gods] lo! I am afraid, and I have pity on thee. But, if thou continue thus, those gods be my witnesses that I will have no pity on thee!

Sharbil said: As a man who art afraid of the emperors and tremblest at idols, have thou no pity on me. For, as for me, I know not what thou sayest: therefore also is my mind not shaken or terrified by those things which thou sayest. For by thy judgments shall all they escape from the judgment to come who do not worship that which is not God in its own nature.

The judge said: Let him be scourged with thongs,[1] because he has dared to answer me thus, and has resisted the command of the emperors, and has not appreciated the honour which the gods conferred on him: inasmuch as, lo! he has renounced them.—And he was scourged by ten [men], who laid hold on him, according to the command of the judge.

Sharbil said: Thou art not aware of the scourging of justice in that world which is to come. For thou wilt cease, and thy judgments also will pass away; but justice will not pass away, nor will its retributions come to an end.

The judge[2] said: Thou art so intoxicated with this same Christianity, that thou dost not even know[3] before whom thou art being judged, and by whom it is that thou art being scourged—[even] by those who formerly held thee in honour, and paid adoration to thy priesthood in the gods. Why dost thou hate honour, and love this ignominy? For, although

---

[1] The Syriac is ܛܘܪܝܣ (*toris*), and is a foreign word, probably the Latin *loris*, which the Syriac translator, not understanding it or not having an equivalent, may have written *loris*, and a subsequent transcriber have written *toris*. It is plain that the later copyist to whom the text B. is due did not know what is meant: for he has omitted the word, and substituted "Sharbil."

[2] B. reads "governor" (ἡγεμών), and so generally in the corresponding places below.

[3] B. reads "discern."

thou speakest contrary to the law, yet I myself cannot turn aside from the laws of the emperors.

Sharbil said: As *thou* takest heed not to depart from the laws of the emperors, and if moreover thou depart [from them] thou knowest what command they will give concerning thee, so do I also take heed not to decline from the law of Him who said, "Thou shalt not worship any image, nor any likeness;" and therefore will I not sacrifice to idols made [with hands]: for long enough was the time in which I sacrificed to them, when I was in ignorance.

The judge said: Bring not upon thee punishment[1] in addition to the punishment which thou hast [already] brought upon thee. Enough is it for thee to have said, "I will not sacrifice:" do not [further] dare to insult the gods, by calling them idols made [with hands]—[gods] whom even the emperors honour.

Sharbil said: But, if on behalf of the emperors, who are far away and not near at hand and not conscious of those who treat their commands with contempt, thou biddest me sacrifice, how is it that on behalf of idols, who lo! are present and are seen, but see not, thou biddest me sacrifice? Why, hereby thou hast declared before all thy attendants[2] that, because they have a mouth and speak not, lo! thou art become a pleader for them: [gods] "to whom their makers shall be like," and "every one that trusteth upon them" [shall be] like thee.

The judge said: It was not for this that thou wast called before me—that, instead of [paying] the honour which is due, thou shouldst despise the emperors. But draw near to the gods and sacrifice, and have pity on thyself, thou self-despiser!

Sharbil said: Why should it be requisite for thee to ask me many questions, after that which I have said to thee: "I will not sacrifice?" Thou hast called me a self-despiser?

---

[1] [Or "judgment."]

[2] The word used is the Latin "officium" [= officiales, or corpus officialium], which denoted the officers that attended upon presidents and chief magistrates. The equivalent Gk. τάξις is used below, p. 93.

But would that from my childhood I had had this mind, and had thus despised myself,[1] which was perishing!

The judge said: Hang him up, and tear him with combs on his sides.—And while he was being torn he cried aloud and said: [It is] for the sake of Christ, who has secretly caused His light to arise upon the darkness of my mind. And, when he had thus spoken, the judge commanded again that he should be torn with combs on his face.

Sharbil said: It is better that *thou* shouldest inflict tortures upon me for not sacrificing, than that I should be judged *there* for having sacrificed to the work of men's hands.

The judge said: Let his body be bent backwards, and [for this purpose] let straps be tied to his hands and his feet; and, when he has been bent backwards, let him be scourged on his belly.—And they scourged him in this manner, according to the command of the judge. Then he commanded that he should go up to the prison, and that he should [there] be cast into a dark dungeon. And the executioners,[2] and the Christians who had come up with him from the church, carried him, because he was not able to walk upon his feet in consequence of his having been bent backwards. And he was in the gaol many days.

But on the second of Ilul,[3] on the third day of the week, the judge arose and went down to his judgment-hall by night; and the whole body of his attendants was with him; and he commanded the keeper of the prison, and they brought him before him. And the judge said to him: [All] this long while hast thou been in prison: what has been thy determination concerning those things on which thou wast questioned before me? Dost thou consent to minister to the gods according to thy former custom, agreeably to the command of the emperors?

Sharbil said: This has been my determination in the prison, that that with which I began before thee, I will [go on

---

[1] [Or "soul."]

[2] The Latin "quæstionarii," [those who officiated at a "quæstio," or examination by torture].

[3] *i.e.* Heb. אֱלוּל, from the new moon of September to that of October.

with and] finish even to the last; nor will I play false with my word. For I will not again confess idols, which I have renounced; nor will I renounce the King Christ, whom I have confessed.

The judge said: Hang him up by his right hand, because he has withdrawn it from the gods that he may not again offer incense with it, until his hand with which he ministered to the gods be dislocated, because he persists in this saying of his.—And, while he was suspended by his hand, they asked him and said to him: Dost thou consent to sacrifice to the gods? But he was not able to return them an answer, on account of the dislocation of his arm. And the judge commanded, and they loosed him and took him down. But he was not able to bring his arm up to his side, until the executioners pressed it and brought it up to his side.

The judge said: Put on incense, and go whithersoever thou wilt, and no one shall compel thee to be a priest again. But, if thou wilt not [do so], I will show thee [tortures] bitterer than these.

Sharbil said: [As for] gods that made not the heavens and the earth, may they perish from under these heavens! But thou, menace me not with words of threatening; but, instead of words, show upon me the deeds of threatening, that I hear thee not again making mention of the detestable name of gods!

The judge said: Let him be branded with the brand of bitter fire between his eyes and upon his cheeks.—And the executioners did so, until the smell of the branding reeked forth in the midst of the judgment-hall: but he refused to sacrifice.

Sharbil said: Thou hast heard for thyself from me, when I said to thee "Thou art not aware of the smoke of the roasting of the fire which is prepared for those who, like thee, confess idols made [by hands], and deny the living God, after thy fashion."

The judge said: Who taught thee all these things, that thou shouldest speak before me thus—a man who wast [once] a friend of the gods and an enemy of Christ, whereas lo! thou art become his advocate?

Sharbil said: Christ whom I have confessed, He it is that hath taught me to speak thus. But there needeth not that I should be His advocate, for His own mercies are eloquent advocates for guilty ones like me, and these will avail to plead[1] on my behalf in the day when the eternal sentences shall be [passed].

The judge said: Let him be hanged up, and let him be torn with combs upon his former wounds; also let salt and vinegar be rubbed into the wounds upon his sides. Then he said to him: Renounce not the gods whom thou didst [formerly] confess.

Sharbil said: Have pity on me [and spare me] again from saying that there be gods, and powers, and fates, and nativities. On the contrary, I confess one God, who made the heavens, and the earth, and the seas, and all that is therein; and the Son who is from Him, the King Christ.

The judge said: It is not about this that thou art questioned before me—[viz.:] what is the belief of the Christians which thou hast confessed; but this [is what] I said to thee, "Renounce not those gods to whom thou wast made priest."

Sharbil said: Where is that [vaunted] wisdom of thine and of the emperors of whom thou makest thy boast, that ye worship the work of the hands of the artificers and confess them, whilst the artificers themselves, who made the idols, ye insult by the burdens and imposts which ye lay upon them? The artificer standeth up at thy presence, to do honour to *thee;* and thou standest up in the presence of the work of the artificer, and dost honour it and worship it.

The judge said: Thou art not the man to call [others] to account for[2] these things; but from thyself a strict account is demanded, as to the cause for which thou hast renounced the gods, and refusest to offer them incense like thy fellow-priests.

Sharbil said: Death on account of this is true life: those who confess the King Christ, He also will confess before His glorious Father.

[1] [Lit. "to be a plea."]   [2] [Or "thou art not the avenger of."]

The judge said: Let lighted candles[1] be brought, and let them be passed round about his face and about the sides of his wounds. And they did so a long while.

Sharbil said: It is well that thou burnest me with this fire, that [so] I may be delivered from "that fire which is not quenched, and the worm that dieth not," which is threatened to those[2] who worship things made instead of the Maker: for it is forbidden to the Christians to honour or worship anything except the nature of Him who is God Most High. For that which is made and is created is [designed to be] a worshipper of its Maker, and is not [itself] to be worshipped along with its Creator, as thou supposest.

The governor said: It is not this for which the emperors have ordered me to demand an account at thy hands, whether there be judgment and the rendering of an account after the death of men; nor yet about *this* do I care, whether that which is made is to be honoured or not to be honoured. What the emperors have commanded *me* is this: that, whosoever will not sacrifice to the gods and offer incense to them, I should employ against him stripes, and combs, and sharp swords.

Sharbil said: The kings of this world are conscious of this world only; but the King of all kings, He hath revealed and shown to us that there is another world, and a judgment in reserve, in which a recompense will be made, on the one hand to those who have served God, and on the other to those who have not served Him nor confessed Him. Therefore do I cry aloud, that I will not again sacrifice to idols, nor will I offer oblations to devils, nor will I do honour to demons!

The judge said: Let nails of iron be driven in between the eyes of the insolent [fellow], and let him go to that world which he is looking forward to, like a fanatic[3] [as he

---

[1] [Lit. "candles of fire."]

[2] The passage from this place to "in the eyes," below, is lost in A., and supplied from B.

[3] Or "dealer in fables," if the word employed here, which is a foreign one, be the Latin "fabularius," which is not certain.

is]. And the executioners did so, the sound of the driving in of the nails being heard as they were being driven in sharply.

Sharbil said: Thou hast driven in nails between my eyes, even as nails were driven into the hands of the glorious Architect of the creation, and by reason of this did all orders of the creation tremble and quake at that season. For these tortures which lo! thou art inflicting on me are [as] nothing in view of that judgment which is to come. For [as for] those "whose ways are always firm," because "they have not the judgment of God before their eyes,"[1] and [who] on this account do not even confess that God exists—neither will He confess them.

The judge said: *Thou* sayest in words that there is a judgment; but I will show thee in deeds: so that, instead of [fearing] that judgment which is to come, thou mayest tremble and be afraid of this one which is before thine eyes, in which lo! thou art involved, and not multiply thy speech before me.

Sharbil said: Whosoever is resolved to set God before his eyes in secret, God will also be at his right hand; and [therefore] I too am not afraid of thy threats of tortures, with which thou dost menace me and seek to make me afraid.

The judge said: Let Christ, whom thou hast confessed, deliver thee from all the tortures which I have inflicted on thee, and am about further to inflict on thee; and let Him show His deliverance towards thee openly, and save thee out of my hands.

Sharbil said: This is the true deliverance of Christ [imparted] to me—this secret power which He has given me to endure all the tortures thou art inflicting on me, and whatsoever it is settled in thy mind still further to inflict upon me; and, although thou hast plainly seen [it to be] so, thou hast refused to credit my word.

The judge said: Take him away from before me, and let him be hanged upon a beam the contrary way, head downwards; and let him be beaten with whips while he is hang-

[1] [Ps. x. 5.]

ing.—And the executioners did so to him, at the door of the judgment-hall.

Then the governor commanded, and they brought him in before him. And he said to him: Sacrifice to the gods, and do the will of the emperors, thou priest that hatest honour and lovest ignominy instead!

Sharbil said: Why dost thou again repeat thy words, and command me to sacrifice, after the many [times] that thou hast heard from me that I will not sacrifice again? For it is not any *compulsion* on the part of the Christians that has kept me back from sacrifices, but the truth they hold: this it is that has delivered me from the error of paganism.

The judge said: Let him be put into a chest[1] of iron like a murderer, and let him be scourged with thongs like a malefactor.—And the executioners did so, until there remained not a sound place on him.

Sharbil said: [As for] these tortures, which thou supposest to be bitter, out of the midst of their bitterness will spring up for me fountains of deliverance and mercy in the day of the eternal sentences.

The governor said: Let small round pieces of wood be placed between the fingers of his hands,[2] and let these be squeezed upon them vehemently.[3]—And they did so to him, until the blood came out from under the nails of his fingers.

Sharbil said: If thine eye be not [yet] satisfied with the tortures of the body, add still further to its tortures whatsoever thou wilt.

The judge said: Let the fingers of his hands be loosed, and make him sit upon the ground; and bind his hands upon

---

[1] [So Cureton. Dr. Payne Smith remarks: "Cureton's 'chest' is a guess from ܩܐܘܕܐ. The only sense of ܩܐܕ with which I am acquainted is *cadus*, a cask." The word occurs again in the *Martyrdom of Habib*. In both places it seems to refer to some contrivance for *holding fast* the person to be scourged. The root appears to be ܩܐܕ, *custodivit, retinuit* (Castel).]

[2] The martyr Minias, about A.D. 240, had the same [?] torture inflicted on him: "ligneis verubus præacutis sub ungues ejus infixis, omnes digitos ejus præcepit pertundi." See Surius, *Sanctt. Vit.*

[3] [Or "bitterly."]

his knees, and thrust a piece of wood under his knees, and let it pass over the bands of his hands, and hang him up by his feet, [thus] bent, head downwards; and let him be scourged with thongs.—And they did so to him.

Sharbil said: They cannot conquer who fight against God, nor may they be overcome whose confidence is God; and therefore do I say, that "neither fire nor sword, nor death nor life, nor height nor depth, can separate my heart from the love of God, which is in our Lord Jesus Christ."

The judge said: Make hot a ball of lead and of brass, and place it under his armpits.—And they did so, until his ribs began to be seen.

Sharbil said: The tortures thou dost inflict upon me are too little for thy rage against me—unless thy rage were little and thy tortures were great.

The judge said: Thou wilt not hurry me on by these things which thou sayest; for I have room in my mind[1] to bear long [with thee], and to behold every evil and shocking and bitter thing which[2] I shall exhibit in the torment of thy body, because thou wilt not consent to sacrifice to the gods whom thou didst [formerly] worship.

Sharbil said: [Even] those things which I have said and repeated before thee, thou in thine unbelief knowest not how to hear: now, [then], supposest thou that thou knowest those things which are in my mind?

The judge said: The answers which thou givest will not help thee, but will [rather] multiply upon thee inflictions manifold.

Sharbil said: If the several stories of thy several gods are by thee accepted as true, [yet] is it matter of shame to us to tell of what sort they are. For one had intercourse with boys, which is not right; and another fell in love with a maiden, who fled for refuge into a tree, as your shameful stories tell.

The judge said: This [fellow], who was formerly a respecter of the gods, but has now turned to insult them and

---

[1] Here a few lines have been torn out of A., and are supplied from B.
[2] ["Which" is not in the printed text.]

has not been afraid, and has also despised the command of the emperors and has not trembled—set him to stand upon a gridiron[1] heated with fire.—And the executioners did so, until the under part of his feet was burnt off.

Sharbil said: If thy rage is excited at [the mention of] the abominable and obscene tales of thy gods, how much more does it become thee to be ashamed of their acts! For lo! if a person were to do what one of thy gods did, and they were to bring him before thee, thou wouldest pass sentence of death upon him.

The judge said: This day will I bring thee to account for thy blasphemy against the gods, and thine audacity in insulting also the emperors; nor will I leave thee alone until thou offer incense to them, according to thy former custom.

Sharbil said: Stand by thy threats, then, and speak not falsely; and show towards me in deeds the authority of the emperors which they have given thee; and do not thyself bring reproach on the emperors with thy falsehood, and be thyself also despised in the eyes of thine attendants!

The judge said: Thy blasphemy against the gods and thine audacity towards the emperors have brought upon thee these tortures which thou art undergoing; and, if thou add further to thine audacity, there shall be further added to thee inflictions bitterer than these.

Sharbil said: Thou hast authority, as judge: do whatsoever thou wilt, and show no pity.

The judge said: How can he that hath had no pity on his own body, so as to avoid suffering in it these tortures, be afraid or ashamed of not obeying the command of the emperors?

Sharbil said: Thou hast well said that I am not ashamed: because near at hand is He that justifieth me, and my soul is caught up in rapture towards Him. For, whereas I

---

[1] The word used looks like a corruption of the Latin *craticula*. Eusebius. *Hist. Eccl.* v. 1, uses the Gk. word for this (τήγανον) in describing the martyrdom of Attalus, who " was set in the τήγανον, and scorched all over, till the savour of his burnt flesh ascended from his body."

[aforetime] provoked Him to anger by the sacrifices of idols, I am this day pacifying Him by the inflictions [I endure] in my person: for my soul is a captive to God who became man.

The judge said: It is a captive, then, that I am questioning, and a madman without sense; and with a dead man who is burnt, lo! am I talking.

Sharbil said: If thou art assured that I am mad, question me no further: for it is a madman that is being questioned; nay, rather, I am a dead man who is burnt, as thou hast said.

The judge said: How shall I count thee a dead man, when lo! thou hast cried aloud, "I will not sacrifice?"

Sharbil said: I myself, too, know not how to return thee an answer, since thou hast called me a dead man and [yet] turnest to question me again as if [I were] alive.

The judge said: Well have I called thee a dead man, because thy feet are burnt and thou carest not, and thy face is scorched and thou holdest thy peace, and nails are driven in between thine eyes and thou takest no account of it, and thy ribs are seen between the [wounds inflicted by the] combs and thou insultest the emperors, and thy whole body is mangled and maimed with stripes and thou blasphemest against the gods; and, because thou hatest thy body, lo! thou sayest whatsoever pleaseth thee.

Sharbil said: If thou callest *me* audacious because I have endured these things, it is fit that thou, who hast inflicted them upon me, shouldest be called a murderer in thy acts and a blasphemer in thy words.

The judge said: Lo! thou hast insulted the emperors, and likewise the gods; and lo! thou [now] insultest me also, in order that I may pronounce sentence of death upon thee quickly. But instead of this, which thou lookest for, I am prepared yet further to inflict upon thee bitter and severe tortures.

Sharbil said: Thou knowest what I have said to thee many times: instead of denunciations of threatening, proceed to show upon me the performance of the threat, that thou mayest be known to do the will of the emperors.

The judge said: Let him be torn with combs upon his

legs and upon the sides of his thighs.—And the executioners did so, until his blood flowed and ran down upon the ground.

Sharbil said: Thou hast well done in treating me thus: because I have heard that one of the teachers of the church hath said, "Scars [are] on my body, that I may come to the resurrection from the place of the dead." Me too, who was a dead man out of sight, lo! thine inflictions bring to life again.

The judge said: Let him be torn with combs on his face, since he is not ashamed of the nails which are driven in between his eyes. And they tore him with combs upon his cheeks, and between the nails which were driven into them.

Sharbil said: I will not obey the emperors, who command that to be worshipped and honoured which is not of the nature of God, and is not God in its nature, but is the work of him that made it.

The judge said: Like as the emperors worship, so also worship thou; and that honour which the judges render, do thou render also.

Sharbil said: Even though *I* insult that which is the work of men and has no perception and no feeling of anything, [yet] do not *thou* insult God, the Maker of all, nor worship along with Him that which is not of Him, and is foreign to His nature.

The judge said: Does this your doctrine so teach you, that you should insult the very luminaries which give light to all the regions of the earth?

Sharbil said: Although it is not enjoined upon us to insult them, yet it is enjoined upon us not to worship them nor honour them, seeing that they are things made: for this were an insufferable [1] wrong, that a thing made should be worshipped along with its Maker; and it is an insult to the Maker that His creatures should be honoured along with Himself.

The judge said: Christ whom thou confessest was hanged on a tree; and on a tree will I hang thee, like thy Master.—And they hanged him on a tree [2] a long while.

[1] [Or "bitter."]   [2] [Or "beam."]

Sharbil said: [As for] Christ, whom lo! thou mockest—see how thy many gods were unable to stand before Him: for lo! they are despised and rejected, and are made a laughing-stock and a jest by those who used formerly to worship them.

The judge said: How is it that thou renouncest the gods, and confessest Christ, who was hanged on a tree?

Sharbil said: This cross of Christ is the great boast of the Christians, since it is by this that the deliverance of salvation has come to all His worshippers, and by this that they have had their eyes enlightened, so as not to worship creatures along with the Creator.

The governor said: Let thy boasting of the cross be kept within thy own mind, and let incense be offered by thy hands to the gods.

Sharbil said: Those who have been delivered by the cross cannot any longer worship and serve the idols of error made [with hands]: for creature cannot worship creature, because it is itself also [designed to be] a worshipper of Him who made it; and that it should be worshipped along with its Maker is an insult to its Maker, as I have said before.

The governor said: Leave alone thy books which have taught thee [to speak] thus, and perform the command of the emperors, that thou die not by the emperors' law.

But Sharbil said: Is this, then, the justice of the emperors, in whom thou takest such pride, that we should leave alone the law of God and keep their laws?

The governor said: The citation of the books in which thou believest, and from which thou hast quoted—it is this which has brought upon thee these afflictions: for, if thou hadst offered incense to the gods, great would have been thine honour, like as it was formerly, as priest of the gods.

Sharbil said: To thine unbelieving heart these things seem as if they were afflictions; but to the true heart "affliction imparts patience, and from it [comes] also experience, and from experience likewise the hope",[1] of the confessor.[2]

The governor said: Hang him up and tear him with combs upon his former wounds.—And, from the fury with

[1] [Rom. v. 4.] [2] [Lit. "of confessorship."]

which the judge urged on the executioners, his very bowels were almost seen. And, lest he should die under the combs and escape from still further tortures, he gave orders and they took him down.

And, when the judge saw that he was become silent and was not able to return him any further answer, he refrained from him a little while, until he began to revive.

Sharbil said: Why hast thou had pity upon me for even this little time, and kept me back from the gain of a confessor's death?[1]

The governor said: I have not had pity on thee at all in refraining for a little while: thy silence it was that made me pause a little; and, if I had power [to go] beyond the law of the emperors, I should like to lay [other] tortures upon thee, so as to be more fully avenged on thee for thine insult toward the gods: for in despising me thou hast despised the gods; and I, on my part, have borne with thee and tortured thee thus, as a man who so deserves [at my hands].

And the judge gave orders, and suddenly the curtain[2] fell before him for a short time; and he settled and drew up the sentence[3] which he should pronounce against him publicly.

And suddenly the curtain was drawn back again; and the judge cried aloud and said: As regards this Sharbil, who was formerly priest of the gods, but has turned this day and renounced the gods, and has cried aloud "I am a Christian," and has not trembled at the gods, but has insulted them; and, further, has not been afraid of the emperors [and] their command; and, though I have bidden him sacrifice to the gods according to his former custom, has not sacrificed, but has treated them with the greatest insult: I have looked [into the matter] and decided, that towards a man who doeth these things, even though he were [now] to sacrifice, it is not fit that any mercy should be shown; and that it is not fit that he should [any longer] behold

---

[1] [Lit. "of confessorship."]
[2] The Latin "velum," or rather its plur. "vela."
[3] The Gk. ἀπόφασις.

the sun of his lords, because he has scorned their laws. I give sentence that, according to the law of the emperors, a strap[1] be thrust into the mouth of the insulter, as into the mouth of a murderer, and that he depart outside of the city of the emperors with haste, as one who has insulted the lords of the city and the gods who hold authority over it. I give sentence that he be sawn with a saw of wood, and that, when he is near to die, then his head be taken off with the sword of the headsmen.

And forthwith a strap was thrust into his mouth with all speed, and the executioners hurried him off, and made him run quickly upon his burnt feet, and took him away outside of the city, a crowd of people running after him. For they had been standing looking on at his trial all day, and wondering that he did not suffer under his afflictions: for his countenance, which was cheerful, testified to the joy of his heart. And, when the executioners arrived at the place where he was to receive the punishment of death, the people of the city were with them, that they might see whether they did according as the judge had commanded, and hear what Sharbil might say at that season, so that they might inform the judge of the country.

And they offered him some wine to drink, according to the custom of murderers to drink. But he said to them: I will not drink, because I wish to feel the saw with which ye saw me, and the sword which ye pass over my neck; but instead of this wine, which will not be of any use to me, give me a little time to pray, while ye stand. And he stood up, and looked toward the east,[2] and lifted up his voice and said: Forgive me, Christ, all the sins I have committed against Thee, and all [the instances in] which I have provoked Thee to anger by the polluted sacrifices of dead idols; and have pity on me and save me,[3] and deliver me from the judgment to come; and be merciful to me, as Thou wast

---

[1] The expression χαλινὸν ἐμβαλεῖν is used similarly in the life of Euthymus in *Eccl. Græc. Monumenta*, vol. ii. p. 240.

[2] [See *Teaching of the Apostles*, Ordinance 1, p. 38.]

[3] [Lit. "have pity on my salvation."]

merciful to the robber; and receive me like the penitents who have been converted and have turned to Thee, as Thou also hast turned to them; and, whereas I have entered into Thy vineyard, [though] at the eleventh hour, instead of judgment, deliver me from justice: let Thy death, which was for the sake of sinners, restore to life again my slain body in the day of Thy coming. And, when the Sharirs of the city heard these things, they were very angry with the executioners for having given him leave to pray.

And, while the nails were [still] remaining which had been driven in between his eyes, and his ribs were seen between the [wounds of the] combs, and while from the burning on his sides and the soles of his feet, which were scorched and burnt, and from the [wounds of the] combs on his face, and on his sides, and on his thighs, and on his legs, the blood was flowing and running down, they brought carpenters' instruments, and thrust him into a wooden vice, and tightened it upon him until the bones of his joints creaked with the pressure; then they put upon him a saw of iron, and began sawing him asunder; and, when he was just about to die, because the saw had reached to his mouth, they smote him with the sword and took off his head, while he was still squeezed down in the vice.

And Babai his sister drew near and spread out her skirt and caught his blood; and she said to him: May my spirit be united with thy spirit in the presence of Christ, whom thou hast known and believed.

And the Sharirs of the city ran and came and informed the judge of the things which Sharbil had uttered in his prayer, and how his sister had caught his blood. And the judge commanded them to return and give orders to the executioners that, on the spot where she had caught the blood of her brother, she also should receive the punishment of death. And the executioners laid hold on her, and each one of them severally put her to torture; and, with her brother's blood upon her, her soul took its flight from her, and they mingled her blood with his. And, when the executioners were entered into the city, the brethren and young men[1] ran and stole away their two corpses; and they laid them in the burial-place of the father of Abshelama the bishop, on the fifth of Ilul, the eve [of the Sabbath].

I wrote these Acts on paper—I, Marinus, and Anatolus, the notaries; and we placed them in the archives of the city, where the papers of the kings are placed.[2]

[This Barsamya,[3] the bishop, made a disciple of Sharbil the priest. And he lived in the days of Binus,[4] bishop of Rome; in whose days the whole population of Rome assembled together, and cried out to the prætor[5] of their city, and said to him: There are too many strangers in this our city, and these cause famine and dearness of everything: but we beseech thee to command them to depart out of the city. And, when he had commanded them to depart out of the city, these strangers assembled themselves together, and said to the prætor: We beseech thee, my lord, command also that the bones of our dead may depart with us. And he commanded them to take the bones of their dead, and to depart. And all the strangers assembled themselves together to take the bones of Simon Cephas and of Paul, the apostles; but the people of Rome said to them: We will not give you the bones of the apostles. And the strangers said to them: Learn ye and understand that Simon, who is called Cephas, is of Bethsaida of Galilee, and Paul the apostle is of Tarsus, a city of Cilicia. And, when the people of Rome knew that this matter was so, then they let them

---

[1] By a transposition of letters, B. reads "laics."

[2] B. has several lines here in addition.

[3] The passage hence to the end is evidently a later addition by a person unacquainted with chronology: for it is stated at the beginning of these Acts that the transactions took place in the fifteenth year of Trajan, A.D. 112; but Fabianus (see next note) was not made bishop of Rome till the reign of Maximinus Thrax, about the year 236.

[4] B. reads "Fabianus:" in A. the first syllable, or rather letter, has been dropped.—The mention of Fabianus probably arose from the fact of his having instituted notaries for the express purpose of searching for and collecting the Acts of Martyrs.

[5] [The Greek $\H{\epsilon}\pi\alpha\rho\chi o\varsigma$.]

alone. And, when they had taken them up and were removing them from their places, immediately there was a great earthquake, and the buildings of the city were on the point of falling down, and [the city] was near being overthrown. And, when the people of Rome saw it, they turned and besought the strangers to remain in their city, and that the bones might be laid in their places [again]. And, when the bones of the apostles were returned to their places, there was quietness, and the earthquakes ceased, and the winds became still, and the air became bright, and the whole city became cheerful. And, when the Jews and pagans saw it, they also ran and fell at the feet of Fabianus, the bishop of their city, the Jews crying out: We confess Christ, whom we crucified: He is the Son of the living God, of whom the prophets spoke in their mysteries. And the pagans also cried out and said to him: We renounce idols and carved images, which are of no use, and we believe in Jesus the King, the Son of God, who has come and is to come again. And, whatever other doctrines there were in Rome and in all Italy, [the followers of] these also renounced their doctrines, like as the pagans had renounced theirs, and confessed the gospel of the apostles, which was preached in the church.]

[Here] end the Acts of Sharbil the confessor.

FURTHER, THE MARTYRDOM OF BARSAMYA,[1] THE BISHOP OF THE BLESSED CITY EDESSA.

In the year four hundred and sixteen of the kingdom of the Greeks, that is the fifteenth year of the reign of the sovereign ruler, our lord, Trajan Cæsar, in the consulship of Commodus and Cyrillus,[2] in the month Ilul, on the fifth day of the month,

[1] This is taken from the MS. cited as B. in the *Acts of Sharbil*. There is an Armenian version or extract of this still in existence: see Dr. Alishan's letter referred to on p. 35.

[2] This is a mistake for Cerealis, and the consulate meant must be that

the day after Lysinus,[1] the judge of the country, had heard [the case of] Sharbil the priest; as the judge was sitting in his judgment-hall, the Sharirs of the city came before him and said to him: We give information before thine Excellency concerning Barsamya, the leader of the Christians, that he went up to Sharbil, the priest, as he was standing and ministering before the venerable gods, and sent and called him to him secretly, and spoke to him, [quoting] from the books in which he reads in the church where their congregation meets, and recited to him the belief of the Christians, and said to him, " It is not right for thee to worship many gods, but [only] one God, and His Son Jesus Christ "—until he made him a disciple, and induced him to renounce the gods whom he had formerly worshipped; and by means of Sharbil himself also many have become disciples, and are gone down to the church, and lo! this day they confess Christ; and even Avida, and Nebo,[2] and Barcalba, and Hafsai, honourable and chief persons of the city, have yielded to Sharbil in this. We, accordingly, as Sharirs of the city, make [this] known before thine Excellency, in order that we may not receive punishment as offenders for not having declared before thine Excellency the things which were spoken in secret to Sharbil by Barsamya the guide of the church. Thine Excellency now knoweth what it is right to command in respect of this said matter.

And, immediately that the judge heard these things, he sent the Sharirs of the city, and some of his attendants with them, to go down to the church and bring up Barsamya from the church. And they led him and brought him up to the judgment-hall of the judge; and there went up many Christians with him, saying: We also will die with Barsamya, because we too are of one mind with him in respect to the doctrine of which he made Sharbil a disciple, and in

of Commodus Verus and Tutilius Cerealis, which was in the ninth (not fifteenth) year of Trajan, which agrees with the 416th year of the Greeks, or A.D. 105.

[1] See note on p. 61.
[2] Called Labu at p. 61.

all that he spoke to him, and in all [the instruction] that Sharbil received from him, so that he was persuaded by him, and died for the sake of that which he heard from him.

And the Sharirs of the city came, and said to the judge: Barsamya, as thine Excellency commanded, lo! is standing at the door of the judgment-hall of thy Lordship;[1] and honourable chief-persons of the city, who became disciples along with Sharbil, lo! are standing by Barsamya, and crying out, "We will all die with Barsamya, who is our teacher and guide."

And, when the judge heard those things which the Sharirs of the city had told him, he commanded them to go out and write down the names of the persons who were crying out, "We will die with Barsamya." And, when they went out to write down [the names of] these persons, those who so cried out were too many for them, and they were not able to write down their names, because they were so many: for the cry kept coming to them from all sides, that they "would die for Christ's sake along with Barsamya."

And, when the tumult of the crowd became great, the Sharirs of the city turned back, and came in to the judge, and said to him: We are not able to write down the names of the persons who are crying aloud outside, because they are too many to be numbered. And the judge commanded that Barsamya should be taken up to the prison, so that the crowd might be dispersed which was collected together about him, lest through the tumult of the multitude there should be some mischief in the city. And, when he went up to the gaol, those who had become disciples along with Sharbil continued with him.

And after many days were passed the judge rose up in the morning and went down to his judgment-hall, in order that he might hear [the case of] Barsamya. And the judge commanded, and they brought him from the prison; and he came in and stood before him. The officers said: Lo, he standeth before thine Excellency.

The judge said: Art thou Barsamya, who hast been made

[1] [Lit. "authority."]

ruler and guide of the people of the Christians, and didst make a disciple of Sharbil, who was chief-priest of the gods, and used to worship them?

Barsamya said: It is I who have done this, and I do not deny it; and I am prepared to die for the truth of this.

The judge said: How is it that thou wast not afraid of the command of the emperors, [so] that, when the emperors commanded that every one should sacrifice, thou didst induce Sharbil, when he was standing and sacrificing to the gods and offering incense to them, to deny that which he had confessed, and confess Christ whom he had denied?

Barsamya said: I was assuredly[1] made a shepherd of men, not for the sake of those only who are found, but also for the sake of those who have strayed from the fold of truth, and become food for the wolves of paganism; and, had I not sought to make Sharbil a disciple, at my hands would his blood have been required; and, if he had not listened to me, I should have been innocent of his blood.

The judge said: Now, therefore, since thou hast confessed that it was thou that madest Sharbil a disciple, at thy hands will I require his death; and on this account it is right that thou rather than he shouldest be condemned before me, because by thy hands he has died the horrible deaths of grievous tortures for having abandoned the command of the emperors and obeyed thy words.

Barsamya said: Not to my words did Sharbil become a disciple, but to the word of God which He spoke: "Thou shalt not worship images and the likenesses of men." And it is not I alone that am content to die the death of Sharbil for his confession of Christ, but also all the Christians, members of the church, are likewise eager for this, because they know that they will secure their salvation before God thereby.

The judge said: Answer me not in this manner, like Sharbil thy disciple, lest thine own torments be worse than his; but promise that thou wilt sacrifice before the gods on his behalf.

Barsamya said: Sharbil, who knew not God, I taught to

[1] [See note 3 on p. 15.]

know [Him]: and dost thou bid *me*, who have known God from my youth, to renounce God? God forbid that I should do this thing!

The judge said: Ye have made the whole creation disciples of the teaching of Christ; and lo! they renounce the many gods whom the many worshipped. Give up this way of thinking,[1] lest I make those who are near tremble at thee as they behold thee to-day, and those also that are afar off as they hear of the torments to which thou art condemned.

Barsamya said: If God is the help of those who pray to Him, who is he that can resist them? Or what is the power that can prevail against them? Or thine own threats—what can they do to them: to men who, before thou give commandment concerning them that they shall die, have their death [already] set before their eyes, and are expecting it every day?

The judge said: Bring not the subject of Christ before my judgment-seat; but, instead of this, obey the command of the emperors, who command to sacrifice to the gods.

Barsamya said: Even though we should not lay the subject of Christ before thee, [yet] the sufferings of Christ are portrayed indelibly[2] in the worshippers of Christ; and, even more than thou hearkenest to the commands of the emperors, do we Christians hearken to the commands of Christ the King of kings.

The judge said: Lo! thou hast obeyed Christ and worshipped him up to this day: henceforth obey the emperors, and worship the gods whom the emperors worship.

Barsamya said: How canst thou bid me renounce that in which I was born? when lo! thou didst exact [punishment] for this at the hand of Sharbil, and saidst to him: Why hast thou renounced the paganism in which thou wast born, and confessed Christianity to which thou wast a stranger? Lo! even before I came into thy presence thou didst thyself give testimony [on the matter] beforehand, and saidst to Sharbil: The Christians, to whom thou art gone [over], do not renounce that in which they were born, but continue

---

[1] [Lit. "this mind."] [2] [Lit. "portrayed and fixed."]

in it. Abide, therefore, by the word, which thou hast spoken.

The judge said: Let Barsamya be scourged, because he has rebelled against the command of the emperors, and has caused those also who were obedient to the emperors to rebel with him.

And, when he had been scourged by five [men], he said to him: Reject not the command of the emperors, nor insult the emperors' gods.

Barsamya said: Thy mind is greatly blinded, O judge, and so also is that of the emperors who gave thee authority; nor are the things that are manifest seen by you; nor do ye perceive that lo! the whole creation worships Christ; and thou sayest to me, Do not worship Him, as if I alone worshipped Him—Him whom the watchers[1] above worship on high.

The judge said: But if *ye* have taught *men* to worship Christ, who is it that has persuaded those above to worship Christ?

Barsamya said: Those above have themselves preached, and have taught those below concerning the living worship of the King Christ, seeing that they worship Him, and His Father, together with His divine Spirit.[2]

The judge said: Give up these things which your writings teach you, and which ye teach also to others, and obey those things which the emperors have commanded, and spurn not their laws—lest ye be spurned by means of the sword from the light of this venerable sun.

Barsamya said: The light which passeth away and abideth not is not the true light, but is [only] the similitude of that true light, to whose beams darkness cometh not near, which is reserved and standeth fast for the true worshippers of Christ.

The judge said: Speak not before me of anything [else]

---

[1] [Comp. Dan. iv. 13. This designation was given to angels after the captivity, in which the Jews had become familiar with the doctrine of tutelary deities.]

[2] [Lit. "the Spirit of His Godhead."]

instead of that about which I have asked thee, lest I dismiss thee from life to death, for denying this light which is seen and confessing that which is not seen.

Barsamya said: I cannot leave alone that about which thou askest me, and speak of that about which thou dost not ask me. It was thou that spakest to me about the light of the sun, and I said before thee that there is a light on high which surpasses in its brightness that of the sun which thou dost worship and honour. For an account will be required of thee for worshipping thy fellow[-creature] instead of God thy Creator.

The judge said: Do not insult the very sun, the light of creatures, nor set thou at nought the command of the emperors, nor contentiously resist the lords of the country, who have authority in it.

Barsamya said: Of what avail is the light of the sun to a blind man that cannot see it? For without the eyes of the body, [we know], it is not possible for its beams to be seen. [So] that by this thou mayest know that it is the work of God, forasmuch as it has no power [of its own] to show its light to the sightless.

The judge said: When I have tortured thee as thou deservest, then will I write word about thee to the Imperial government, [reporting] what insult thou hast offered to the gods, in that thou madest a disciple of Sharbil the priest, one who honoured the gods, and that ye despise the laws of the emperors, and that ye make no account of the judges of the countries, and live like barbarians, [though] under the authority of the Romans.

Barsamya said: Thou dost not terrify me by these things which thou sayest. It is true, I am not in the presence of the emperors to-day; yet lo! before the authority which the emperors have given thee I am now standing, and I am brought to trial, because I said, I will not renounce God, to whom the heavens and the earth belong, nor His Son Jesus Christ, the King of all the earth.

The judge said: If thou art indeed assured of this, that thou art standing and being tried before the authority of the emperors, obey their commands, and rebel not against their laws, lest like a rebel thou receive the punishment of death.

Barsamya said: But if those who rebel against the emperors, [even] when they justly rebel, are deserving of death, as thou sayest; for those who rebel against God, the King of kings, even the punishment of death by the sword is too little.

The judge said: It was not that thou shouldest expound in my judgment-hall that thou wast brought in before me, because the trial on which thou standest has but little concern with expounding, but much concern with the punishment of death, for those who insult the emperors and comply not with their laws.

Barsamya said: Because God is not before your eyes, and ye refuse to hear the word of God; and graven images that are of no use, "which have a mouth and speak not," are accounted by you as though they spake, because your understanding is blinded by the darkness of paganism in which ye stand—

The judge [interrupting] said: Leave off those things thou art saying, for they will not help thee at all, and worship the gods, before the bitter [tearings of] combs and harsh tortures come upon thee.

Barsamya said: Do thou [too] leave off the many questions which lo! thou askest me, and [at once] give command for the stripes and the combs with which thou dost menace me: for thy words will not help thee so much as thy inflictions will help me.

The judge said: Let Barsamya be hanged up and torn with combs.

And at that very moment there came to him letters from Alusis[1] the chief proconsul, father of emperors.[2] And he commanded, and they took down Barsamya, and he was not torn with combs; and they took him outside of the hall of judgment.

---

[1] This seems to be *Lusius* Quietus, Trajan's general in the East at this time.

[2] [Or "kings."]

And the judge commanded that the nobles, and the chief persons, and the princes, and the honourable persons of the city, should come before him, that they might hear what was the order that was issued by the emperors, by the hand of the proconsuls, the rulers of the countries under the authority of the Romans. And it was found that the emperors had written by the hand of the proconsuls to the judges of the countries:[1] "Since our Majesty commanded that there should be a persecution against the people of the Christians, we have heard and learned, from the Sharirs whom we have in the countries under the dominion of our Majesty, that the people of the Christians are persons who eschew murder, and sorcery, and adultery, and theft, and bribery and fraud, and those things for which the laws of our Majesty also exact punishment from those who commit them. We, therefore, in our impartial justice, have commanded that on account of these things the persecution of the sword shall cease from them, and that there shall be rest and quietness in all our dominions, they continuing to minister according to their custom and no man hindering them. It is not, however, towards them that we show clemency, but towards their laws, agreeing as they do with the laws of our Majesty. And, if any man hinder them after this our command, that sword which is ordered by us to descend upon those who despise our command, the same do we command to descend upon those who despise this decree of our clemency."

And, when this command of the emperor's clemency was read, the whole city rejoiced that there was quietness and rest for every man. And the judge commanded, and they released Barsamya, that he might go down to his church. And the Christians went up in great numbers to the judgment-hall, together with a great multitude of the population of the city, and they received Barsamya with great and exceeding honour, repeating psalms before him, according to

[1] We have here probably the most authentic copy of the edict of Trajan commanding the stopping of the persecution of the Christians, as it was taken down at the time by the reporters who heard it read.

their custom; [there went] also the wives of the chief of the wise men. And they thronged [about him], and saluted him, and called him "the persecuted confessor," "the companion of Sharbil the martyr." And he said to them: Persecuted I am, like yourselves; but from the tortures and combs of Sharbil and his companions I am clean escaped.[1] And they said to him: We have heard from thee that a teacher of the church has said, "The will, according to what it is, so is it accepted."[2] And, when he was entered into the church, he and all the people that were with him, he stood up and prayed, and blessed them and sent them away to their homes rejoicing and praising God for the deliverance which He had wrought for them and for the church.

And the day after Lysinas[3] the judge of the country had set his hand to these Acts, he was dismissed from his authority.

I Zenophilus and Patrophilus are the notaries who wrote these Acts, Diodorus and Euterpes,[4] Sharirs of the city, bearing witness with us by setting-to their hand, as the ancient laws of the ancient kings command.

[This[5] Barsamya, bishop of Edessa, who made a disciple of Sharbil, the priest of the same city, lived in the days of Fabianus, bishop of the city of Rome. And ordination to the priesthood was received by Barsamya from Abshelama, who was bishop in Edessa; and by Abshelama ordination was received from Palut the First; and by Palut ordination was received from Serapion, bishop of Antioch; and by Serapion ordination was received from Zephyrinus, bishop of Rome; and Zephyrinus of Rome received ordination from Victor of the same place, [viz.] Rome; and Victor received ordination from Eleutherius; and Eleutherius received it from Soter; and Soter received it from

---

[1] [Lit. "am far removed."]
[2] [2 Cor. viii. 12. Both the Peshito and the Greek (if τίς be rejected) have "what it *hath*:" not "what it *is*."]
[3] [See note on p. 61.]   [4] Perhaps "Eutropius."
[5] What follows, down to the end, is a much later addition, evidently made by the same ignorant person as that at p. 79 above: see note there.

Anicetus; and Anicetus received it from Dapius;[1] and Dapius received it from Telesphorus; and Telesphorus received it from Xystus;[2] and Xystus received it from Alexander; and Alexander received it from Evartis;[3] and Evartis received it from Cletus; and Cletus received it from Anus;[4] and Anus received it from Simon Cephas; and Simon Cephas received it from our Lord, together with his fellow-apostles, on the first day of the week, [the day] of the ascension of our Lord to His glorious Father, which was the fourth day of Heziran,[5] which was [in] the nineteenth [6] year of the reign of Tiberius Cæsar, in the consulship of Rufus and Rubelinus, which year was the year 341; for in the year 309 occurred the advent[7] of our Saviour in the world, according to the testimony which we ourselves have found in a correct register [8] among the archives, which errs not at all in whatever it sets forth.]

[Here] endeth the martyrdom of Barsamya, bishop of Edessa.

[1] That is "Pius." The blunder arose from taking the prefix D (?) as a part of the name.

[2] [i.e. "Sixtus."]

[3] [Or "Eortis." The person referred to is "Evaristus." Cureton reads "Erastus:" it does not appear why.]

[4] [i.e. "Linus:" see note on p. 55.]

[5] [See note on p. 36.]

[6] Put by mistake for "sixteenth," which agrees with the statement of Julius Africanus as to the date of our Lord's death; also with the year of the consulate of Rubellius Geminus and Fufius Geminus (the persons intended below), and with the year of the Greeks 341, which was A.D. 29 or 30.

[7] [Prop. "rising," as of the sun.]

[8] The Greek ἀναγραφή: see Du Fresne, *Glossarium*.

MARTYRDOM OF HABIB THE DEACON.[1]

In the month Ab,[2] of the year six hundred and twenty of the kingdom of Alexander the Macedonian, in the consulate of Licinius and Constantine,[3] which is the year in which he[4] was born, in the magistracy[5] of Julius and Barak, in the days of Cona[6] bishop of Edessa, Licinius made a persecution against the church and all the people of the Christians, after that first persecution which Diocletian the emperor had made. And Licinius the emperor commanded that there should be sacrifices and libations, and that the altars in every place should be restored, that they might burn sweet spices and frankincense before Zeus.

And, when many were persecuted, they cried out of their own accord: We are Christians; and they were not afraid of the persecution, because these who were persecuted were more numerous than those who persecuted [them].

Now Habib, who was of the village of Telzeha[7] and had been made a deacon, went secretly into the churches which were in the villages, and ministered and read the Scriptures, and encouraged and strengthened many by his words, and admonished them to stand fast in the truth of their belief, and not to be afraid of the persecutors; and gave them directions [for their conduct].

And, when many were strengthened by his words, and received his addresses affectionately, being careful not to renounce the covenant they had made, and when the Sharirs of the city, the men who had been appointed with reference to this particular matter, heard of it, they went in and in-

---

[1] This is found in the same MS. as the preceding: Cod. Add. 14,645, fol. 238, vers.

[2] [August.]   [3] They were consuls together in A.D. 312, 313, 315.

[4] [It does not appear who is meant.]

[5] The Greek στρατηγία, with a Syriac termination. Στρατηγοί was used for the Latin *Magistratus* or *Duumviri*.

[6] He laid the foundation of the church at Edessa A.D. 313: see Assem. *Bibl. Orient.* vol. i. p. 394.

[7] Called "Thelsæa" by Metaphrastes, *infra*.

formed Lysanias, the governor who was in the town of Edessa, and said to him: Habib, who is a deacon in the village of Telzeha, goes about and ministers secretly in every place, and resists the command of the emperors, and is not afraid.

And, when the governor heard these things, he was filled with rage against Habib; and he made a report, and sent and informed Licinius the emperor of all those things which Habib was doing; [he wished] also to ascertain[1] what command would be issued respecting him and [the rest of] those who would not sacrifice. [For] although a command had been issued that every one should sacrifice, yet it had not been commanded what should be done to those who did not sacrifice: because they had heard that Constantine, the commander[2] in Gaul and Spain, was become a Christian and did not sacrifice. And Licinius the emperor [thus] commanded Lysanias the governor: Whoever it is that has been so daring as to transgress our command, our Majesty has commanded that he shall be burned[3] with fire; and that all others who do not consent to sacrifice shall be put to death by the sword.

Now, when this command came to the town of Edessa, Habib, in reference to whom the report had been made, was gone across [the river] to the country of the people of Zeugma,[4] to minister there also secretly. And, when the governor sent and inquired for him in his village, and in all the country round about, and he was not to be found, he commanded that all his family should be arrested, and also the inhabitants of his village; and they arrested them and put them in irons, his mother and the rest of his family, and also some of the people of his village; and they brought them to the city, and shut them up in prison.

And, when Habib heard what had taken place, he considered

---

[1] [Lit. "learn and see."]
[2] [The word used is probably ἐπαρχικός == *præfectus*: see Dr. Payne Smith, *Thes. Syr.*]
[3] [Dr. Wright's reading, by the change of a letter, for "shall perish."]
[4] [This place was on the right bank of the Euphrates, and derived its name from a bridge of boats laid across the river there. It was about forty miles from Edessa.]

in his mind and pondered anxiously in his thoughts: It is expedient for me, [said he], that I should go and appear before the judge of the country, rather than that I should remain in secret and others should be brought in [to him] and be crowned [with martyrdom] because of me, and that I should find myself in great shame. For in what respect will the name of Christianity help him who flees from the confession of Christianity? Lo! if he flee from this, the death of nature is before him whithersoever he goes, and escape from it he cannot, because this is decreed against all the children of Adam.

And Habib arose and went to Edessa secretly, having prepared his back for the stripes and his sides for the combs, and his person for the burning of fire. And he went immediately[1] to Theotecna,[2] a veteran[3] who was chief of the band of attendants[4] on the governor; and he said to him: I am Habib of Telzeha, whom ye are inquiring for. And Theotecna said to him: If so be that no one saw thee coming to me, hearken to me in what I say to thee, and depart and go away to the place where thou hast been, and remain there in this time [of persecution]; and of this, that thou camest to me and spakest with me and that I advised thee thus, let no one know or be aware. And about thy family and the inhabitants of thy village, be not at all anxious: for no one will at all hurt them; but they will be in prison a few days only, and [then] the governor will let them go: because against *them* the emperors have not commanded anything serious or alarming. But, if on the contrary thou wilt not be persuaded by me in regard to these things which I have said to thee, I am clear of thy blood: because, if so be that thou appear before the judge of the country, thou wilt not escape from death by fire, according to the command of the emperors which they have issued concerning thee.

[1] [Cureton has ܒܠܚܘܕ, which he renders "alone." Dr. Payne Smith considers this a mistake for ܒܡܠܐ.]
[2] In Latin, "Theotecnus."   [3] [Or "an old man."]
[4] The Gk. τάξις here used corresponds to the Latin *officium*. See note on p. 64.

Habib said to Theotecna: It is not about my family and the inhabitants of my village that I am concerned, but for my own salvation, lest it should be forfeited. About this too I am much distressed, that I did not happen to be in my village on the day that the governor inquired for me, and that on my account lo! many are put in irons, and I have been looked upon by him as a fugitive. Therefore, if so be that thou wilt not consent to my request and take me in before the governor, I will go alone and appear before him.

And, when Theotecna heard him speak thus to him, he laid hold of him firmly, and handed him over to his assistants,[1] and they went together to conduct him to the judgment-hall of the governor. And Theotecna went in and informed the governor, and said to him: Habib of Telzeha, whom thine Excellency was inquiring for, is come. And the governor said: Who is it that has brought him? and where did they find him? and what did he do where he was? Theotecna said to him: He came hither himself, of his own accord, and without the compulsion of any one, since no one knew anything about him.

And when the governor heard [this], he was greatly exasperated against him; and thus he spake: This [fellow], who has so acted, has shown great contempt towards me and has despised me, and has accounted me as no judge; and, because he has so acted, it is not meet that any mercy should be shown towards him; nor yet either that I should hasten to pass sentence of death against him, according to the command of the emperors concerning him; but it is meet for me to have patience with him, so that the bitter torments and punishments [inflicted on him] may be the more abundant, and that through him I may terrify many [others] from daring again to flee.

And, many persons being collected together and standing by him at the door of the judgment-hall, some of whom were members of the body of attendants, and some people of the city, there were some of them that said to him: Thou hast done badly in coming and showing thyself to

---

[1] [Or "domestics."]

those who were inquiring for thee, without the compulsion of the judge; and there were [others], again, who said to him: Thou hast done well in coming and showing thyself of thine own accord, rather than that the compulsion of the judge should bring thee: for now is thy confession of Christ known to be of thine own will, and not from the compulsion of men.

And those things which the Sharirs of the city had heard from those who were speaking to him as they stood at the door of the judgment-hall—and this circumstance also in particular, that he had gone secretly to Theotecna and that he had not been willing to denounce him, had been heard by the Sharirs of the city—everything that they had heard they made known to the judge.

And the judge was enraged against those who had been saying to Habib: Wherefore didst thou come and show thyself to the judge, without the compulsion of the judge himself? And to Theotecna he said: It is not seemly for a man who has been made chief over his fellows to act deceitfully in this manner towards his superior, and to set at nought the command of the emperors, which they issued against Habib the rebel, that he should be burned with fire.

Theotecna said: I have not acted deceitfully against my fellows, neither was it my purpose to set at naught the command which the emperors have issued: for what am I before thine Excellency, that I should have dared to do this? But I strictly questioned him as to that for which thine Excellency also has demanded an account at my hands, that I might know and see whether it was of his own free will that he came hither, or whether the compulsion of thine Excellency brought him by the hand of others; and, when I heard from him that he came of his own accord, I carefully brought him to the honourable door of the judgment-hall of thy Worship.[1]

And the governor hastily commanded, and they brought in Habib before him. The officers said: Lo! he standeth before thine Excellency.

[1] [Lit. "rectitude."]

And he began to question him thus, and said to him: What is thy name? And whence art thou? And what art thou?

He said to him: My name is Habib, and I am from the village of Telzeha, and I have been made a deacon.

The governor said: Wherefore hast thou transgressed the command of the emperors, and dost minister in thine office of deacon, which thou art forbidden by the emperors to do, and refusest to sacrifice to Zeus, whom the emperors worship?

Habib said: We are Christians: we do not worship the works of men, who are nothing, whose works also are nothing; but we worship God, who made the men.

The governor said: Persist not in that daring mind with which thou art come into my presence, and insult not Zeus, the great boast of the emperors.

Habib said: But this Zeus is an idol, the work of men. It is very well for thee to say that I insult him. But, if the carving of him out of wood and the fixing of him with nails proclaim aloud concerning him that he is made, how sayest thou to me that I insult him? since lo! his insult is from himself, and against himself.

The governor said: By this very thing, that thou refusest to worship him, thou insultest him.

Habib said: But, if because I do not worship him I insult him, how great an insult, then, did the carpenter inflict on him, who carved him with an axe of iron; and the smith, who smote him and fixed him with nails!

And, when the governor heard him speak thus, he commanded him to be scourged without pity. And, when he had been scourged by five [men], he said to him: Wilt thou now obey the emperors? For, if thou wilt not obey [them], I will tear thee severely with combs, and I will torture thee with all [kinds of] tortures, and then at last I will give command concerning thee that thou be burned with fire.

Habib said: These threats with which lo! thou art seeking to terrify me, are much meaner and paltrier than those which I had already settled it in my mind to endure: therefore[1] came I and made my appearance before thee.

The governor said: Put him into the iron cask[2] for murderers, and let him be scourged as he deserves. And, when he had been scourged, they said to him: Sacrifice to the gods. But he cried aloud, and said: Accursed are your idols, and so are they who join with you in worshipping them like you.

And the governor commanded, and they took him up to the prison; but they refused him permission to speak with his family, or with the inhabitants of his village, according to the command of the judge. On that day was the festival of the emperors.

And on the second of Ilul the governor commanded, and they brought him from the prison. And he said to him: Wilt thou renounce the profession thou hast made[3] and obey the command which the emperors issue? For, if thou wilt not obey, with the bitter tearings of combs will I make thee obey them.

Habib said: I have not obeyed them, and moreover it is settled in my mind that I will not obey them—no, not even if thou lay upon me punishments still worse than those which the emperors have commanded.

The governor said: By the gods I swear, that, if thou do not sacrifice, I will leave no harsh and bitter [sufferings untried] with which I will not torture thee: and we shall see whether Christ, whom thou worshippest, will deliver thee.

Habib said: All those who worship Christ are delivered through Christ, because they worship not creatures along with the Creator of creatures.

The governor said: Let him be stretched out and be scourged with whips, until there remain not a place in his body on which he has not been scourged.

Habib said: [As for] these inflictions, which thou supposest to be [so] bitter with their lacerations,[4] out of them are plaited crowns of victory for those who endure them.

---

[1] [Lit. "then."]   [2] [See note on p. 70.]
[3] [Lit. "Wilt thou renounce that in which thou standest?"]
[4] [Lit. "scourgings."]

The governor said: How call ye afflictions ease, and account the torments of your bodies a crown of victory?

Habib said: It is not for thee to ask me concerning these things, because thine unbelief is not worthy to hear the reasons of them. That I will not sacrifice I have said [already], and I say [so still].

The governor said: Thou art subjected to these punishments because thou deservest them: I will put out thine eyes, which look upon this Zeus and are not afraid of him; and I will stop thine ears, which hear the laws of the emperors and tremble not.

Habib said: To the God whom thou deniest here belongs that other world; and there wilt thou [be made to] confess Him with scourgings, though thou hast again denied Him.

The governor said: Leave alone that world of which thou hast spoken, and consider anxiously now, that from this punishment to which lo! thou art being subjected there is no one that can deliver thee; unless indeed the gods deliver thee, on thy sacrificing to them.

Habib said: Those who die for the sake of the name of Christ, and worship not those objects that are made and created, will "find" their life in the presence of God; but those who love the life of time more than that—their torment will be for ever.

And the governor commanded, and they hanged him up and tore him with combs; and, while they were tearing him with the combs, they knocked him about. And he was hanging a long while, until the shoulderblades of his arms creaked.

The governor said to him: Wilt thou comply even now, and put on incense before Zeus there?[1]

Habib said: Previously to these sufferings I did not comply with thy demands: [and] now that lo! I have undergone them, how thinkest thou that I shall comply, and thereby lose that which I have gained by them?

The governor said: By punishments fiercer and bitterer than these I am prepared to make thee obey, according to the command of the emperors, until thou do their will.

[1] [Pointing to the image.]

Habib said: Thou art punishing me for not obeying the command of the emperors, when lo! thou thyself also, whom the emperors have raised to greatness and made a judge, hast transgressed their command, in that thou hast not done to me that which the emperors have commanded thee.

The governor said: Because I have had patience with thee, [therefore] hast thou spoken thus, like a man that brings an accusation.

Habib said: Hadst thou not scourged me, and bound me, and torn me with combs, and put my feet in fetters,[1] there *would* have been room to think that thou hadst had patience with me. But, if these things take place in the meanwhile, where is the patience towards me of which thou hast spoken?

The governor said: These things which thou hast said will not help thee, because they all go against thee, and they will bring upon thee inflictions bitterer even than those which the emperors have commanded.

Habib said: Had I not been sensible that they would help me, I should not have spoken a single word about them before thee.

The governor said: *I* will silence thy speeches, and at the same time as regards thee pacify the gods, whom thou hast not worshipped; and I will satisfy the emperors in respect to thee, as regards thy rebellion against their commands.

Habib said: I am not afraid of the death with which thou seekest to terrify me; for, had I been afraid of it, I should not have gone about from house to house and ministered: on which account [it was that] I did so minister.[2]

The governor said: How is it that thou worshippest and honourest a man, but refusest to worship and honour Zeus there?

Habib said: I worship not a man, because the Scripture teaches me,[3] " Cursed is every one that putteth his trust in

---

[1] [Or "the stocks." The word is of the most indefinite kind, answering to ξύλον and *lignum*.]

[2] [For this sense, which appears to be the one intended, it is necessary to change ܠܫܡܫܘ into ܐܫܡܫ.]

[3] [Lit. "it is written for me."]

man;" but God, who took upon Him a body and became a man, [Him] do I worship, and glorify.

The governor said: Do thou that which the emperors have commanded; and, as for that which is in thy own mind, if thou art willing to give it up, [well]; but, if thou art not willing, [then] do not abandon it.

Habib said: To do both these things [together] is impossible: because falsehood is contrary to truth, and it is impossible that that should be banished from my thoughts which is firmly fixed in my mind.

The governor said: By inflictions bitter and severe will I make thee dismiss from thy thoughts that of which thou hast said, It is firmly fixed in my mind.

Habib said: [As for] these inflictions by which thou thinkest that it will be rooted out of my thoughts, by means of these it is that it grows within my thoughts, like a tree which bears fruit.

The governor said: What help will stripes and combs give to that tree of thine? and more especially at the time when I shall command fire against it, to burn it up without pity.

Habib said: It is not on those things at which thou lookest that I look, because I contemplate the things which are out of sight; and therefore I do the will of God, the Maker [of all things], and not that of an idol made [with hands], which is not sensible of anything whatever.

The governor said: Because he thus denies the gods whom the emperors worship, let him be torn with combs in addition to his former tearings: for, amidst the many questions which I have had the patience to ask him, he has forgotten his former tearings.

And, while they were tearing him, he cried aloud and said: "The sufferings of this time are not equal to that glory which shall be revealed in"[1] those who love Christ.

And, when the governor saw that even under these inflictions he refused to sacrifice, he said to him: Does your doctrine so teach you, that you should hate your own bodies?

Habib said: Nay, we do not hate our bodies: the Scrip-

[1] [Rom. viii. 18.]

ture distinctly teaches us, "Whosoever shall lose his life shall find it."[1] But another thing too it teaches us: that we should "not cast that which is holy to dogs, nor cast pearls before swine."[2]

The governor said: I know that in speaking thus thy sole object is that my rage and the wrath of my mind may be excited, and that I may pronounce sentence of death against thee speedily. I am not going, then, to be hurried on to that which thou desirest; but I will have patience: not, indeed, for thy relief, but so that the tortures inflicted on thee may be increased, and that thou mayest see thy flesh falling off before thy face by means of the combs that are passing over thy sides.

Habib said: I myself also am looking for this, that thou shouldst multiply thy tortures upon me, even as thou hast said.

The governor said: Submit to the emperors, who have power to do whatsoever they choose.

Habib said: It is not of men to do whatsoever they choose, but of God, whose power is in the heavens, and over all the dwellers upon earth; "nor is there any that may rebuke His hands[3] and say to Him, 'What doest Thou?'"

The governor said: For this insolence of thine, death by the sword is too small [a punishment]. I, however, am prepared to command [the infliction] upon thee of a death more bitter than that of the sword.

Habib said: And I, too, am looking for a death which is more lingering than that of the sword, which thou mayest pronounce upon me at any time thou choosest.

And thereupon the governor proceeded to pass sentence of death upon him. And he called out aloud before his attendants, and said, whilst they were listening to him, as were also the nobles of the city: This Habib, who has denied the gods, as ye have also heard from him, and furthermore has reviled the emperors, deserves that his life should be blotted out from beneath this glorious Sun, and that he should not

---

[1] [Matt. x. 39.]   [2] [Matt. vii. 6.]
[3] [Chaldee, "restrain [lit. smite] His hand." See Dan. iv. 35.]

[any longer] behold this luminary, associate of gods; and, had it not been commanded by former emperors that the corpses of murderers should be buried, it would not be right that the corpse of this [fellow] either should be buried, because he has been so insolent. I command, that a strap be put into his mouth, as into the mouth of a murderer, and that he be burned by a slow lingering fire, so that the torment of his death may be increased.

And he went out from the presence of the governor, with the strap thrust into his mouth; and a multitude of the people of the city ran after him. And the Christians were rejoicing, forasmuch as he had not turned aside nor quitted his post;[1] but the pagans were threatening him, for refusing to sacrifice. And they led him forth by the western archway, over against the cemetery,[2] which was built by[3] Abshelama,[4] the son of Abgar. And his mother was clad in white, and she went out with him.

And, when he was arrived at the place where they were going to burn him, he stood up and prayed, as did all those who came out with him; and he said: "O King Christ, since Thine is this world, and Thine the world to come, behold and see, that, while I might have fled from these afflictions, I did not flee, in order that I might not fall into the hands of Thy justice: may this fire, in which I am to be burned, serve me for a recompense before Thee, so that I may be delivered from that fire which is not quenched; and receive Thou my spirit into Thy presence, through Thy Divine Spirit, O glorious Son of the adorable Father!" And, when he had prayed, he turned and blessed them; and they gave him the salutation, weeping [as they did so], both men and women; and they said to him: Pray for us in the presence of thy Lord, that He would cause peace among His people, and restoration to His churches which are overthrown.

And, while Habib was standing, they dug a place, and

---

[1] [Or "departed from his covenant."]   [2] [The Gk. κοιμητήριον.]

[3] [Cureton's "for" seems not so good, the reference not being to a single tomb.]

[4] Probably that in which Sharbil and Babai were buried: see p. 79 above.

brought him and set him within it; and they fixed up by him a stake. And they came to bind him to the stake; but he said to them: I will not stir from this place in which ye are going to burn me. And they brought fagots, and set them in order, and placed them on all sides of him. And, when the fire blazed up and the flame of it rose fiercely, they called out to him: Open thy mouth. And the moment he opened his mouth his soul mounted up. And they cried aloud, both men and women, with the voice of weeping.

And they pulled and drew him out of the fire, throwing over him fine linen cloths and choice ointments and spices. And they snatched away some of the pieces of wood [which had been put] for his burning, and the brethren and some persons of the laity[1] bore him away. And they prepared him for interment, and buried him by Guria and Shamuna the martyrs, in the same grave in which they were laid, on the hill which is called Baith Allah Cucla,[2] repeating over him psalms and hymns, and conveying his burnt body affectionately and honourably [to the grave]. And even some of the Jews and pagans took part with the Christian brethren in winding up and burying his body. At the time, too, when he was burned, and also at the time when he was buried, there was one spectacle of grief overspreading those within and those without; tears, too, were running down from all eyes: while every one gave glory to God, because for His name's sake he had given his body to the burning of fire.

The day on which he was burned was the eve [of the Sabbath],[3] the second of the month Ilul—the day on which the news came that Constantine the Great had set out from the interior of Spain, to proceed to Rome, the city of Italy, that he might carry on war with Licinius, that [emperor] who at this day rules over the eastern portion of the terri-

---

[1] [Lit. "secular persons," or "men of the world."]

[2] In Simeon Metaphrastes, whose copy would seem to have had a slightly different reading, it is written *Bethelabicla*, and is said to lie on the north side of the city.

[3] [*i.e.* the sixth day of the week. See note on p. 38.]

tories of the Romans; and lo! the countries on all sides are in commotion, because no man knows which of them will conquer and continue in [the possession of] his imperial power. And through this report the persecution slackened for a little while from the church.

And the notaries wrote down everything which they had heard from the judge; and the Sharirs of the city wrote down all the other things which were spoken outside the door of the judgment-hall, and, according to the custom that existed, they reported to the judge all that they had seen and all that they had heard, and the decisions of the judge were written down in their Acts.

I, Theophilus, who have renounced the evil inheritance of my fathers, and confessed Christ, carefully wrote out a copy of these Acts of Habib, even as I had formerly written out [those] of Guria and Shamuna,[1] his fellow-martyrs. And, whereas he had felicitated them upon their death by the sword, he himself also was made like them by the fire in which he was burnt, and received his crown. And, whereas I have written down the year, and the month, and the day, of the coronation of these martyrs, it is not for the sake of those who, like me, were spectators of the deed, but with the view that those who come after us may learn at what time these martyrs suffered, and what manner of men they were; [even as they may learn] also from the Acts of the former martyrs, who [lived] in the days of Domitianus and of all the other emperors who likewise also raised a persecution against the church, and put a great many to death, by stripes and by [tearing with] combs, and by bitter inflictions, and by sharp swords, and by burning fire, and by the terrible sea, and by the merciless mines. And all these things, and things like them, [they suffered] for the hope of the recompense to come.

Moreover, the afflictions of these martyrs, and of those of

---

[1] As Simeon Metaphrastes, *infra*, evidently made use of these *Acts of Habib* in his account of that martyr, it is probable that his narrative of the martyrdom of Guria and Shamuna also was founded on the copy of their "Acts" to which Theophilus here refers.

whom I had heard, opened the eyes of me, Theophilus, and enlightened my mind, and I confessed Christ, that He is the Son of God, and is God. And may the dust of the feet of these martyrs, which I received as I was running after them at the time when they were departing to be crowned, procure me pardon for having denied Him, and may He confess me before His worshippers, seeing that I have confessed Him now!

And at the twenty-seventh question which the judge put to Habib, he gave sentence against him of death by the burning of fire.

[Here] endeth the martyrdom of Habib the deacon.

HOMILY ON HABIB THE MARTYR, COMPOSED BY MAR JACOB.[1]

Habib the martyr, clad in flame, hath called to me out of the fire,
    That for him likewise I should fashion an image of beauty among the glorious.
Comrade of conquerors, lo! he beckoneth to me out of the burning,
    That, as for the glory of his Lord, I should sing concerning him.
In the midst of live coals stands the [heroic] man, and lo! he calleth to me,
    That I should fashion his image: but the blazing fire permits me not.

His love is fervid, glowing is his faith;
    His fire also burneth, and who is adequate to recount his love?
Nay, by reason of that love which led the martyr into the fire,
    No man is able to recount his beauties divine.

---

[1] The MS. from which this is taken is Cod. Add. 17,158, fol. 30 vers. Mar Jacob, bishop of Sarug, or Batnæ, was one of the most learned and celebrated among all the Syriac writers. He was born A.D. 452, made bishop of Sarug A.D. 519, and died A.D. 521. He was the author of several liturgical works, epistles, and sermons, and, amongst these, of numerous metrical homilies, of which two are given here. Assemani enumerates no less than 231. Ephraem Syrus also wrote a similar homily on Habib, Shamuna, and Guria. [The metre of the original in this and the following homily consists of twelve syllables, or six dissyllabic feet; but whether they were read as iambs or trochees, or as

For who shall dare enter and see in the blazing fire
  To whom he is like, and after what pattern he is to be fashioned among the glorious?

Shall I fashion his image by the side of the youths, the children of the furnace?
  With Hananiah shall I reckon Habib? I know not.
Lo! these were not burned there: how, then, is he like?
  He, [I say], like them, when he was burned, and the youths not?
Which, I ask, [the more] beautiful—Habib the martyr, or Azariah?
  Difficult for me is the image: how I am to look upon it, I know not.
Lo! Michael was not burned by the flame;
  But Habib was burned: which, then, [the more] beautiful to him that looketh upon him?
Who shall dare say that this is repulsive, or that;
  Or not so comely this as that, to him that beholdeth him?

Three [there are] in the fire, and the flame cometh not near them;
  But one was burned: and how shall I suffice to tell
That the Fourth [form] is that of Him who went down into the midst of the furnace,
  That He might fashion an image for Habib there along with [those of] the three?
He giveth a place in the fire to him who was burned,
  That he may be, instead of Him the Fourth, by the side of the conquerors.

And, if of the three the beauties be glorious, though they were not burned,
  How shall not this one, who *was* burned, be mingled with the glorious?
If a man have the power either to be burned or not to be burned,
  Of this man, who was burned, more exalted was the beauty than that of the three.
But, inasmuch as of the Lord is the control [of all things],
  He is to be praised, [both] where He rescues and where He delivers up.

both, appears to depend on the nature of the Syriac accentuation, which is still an unsettled question. Hoffmann, in his slight notice of the subject (*Gram. Syr.* § 13), merely says: " Scimus, poësin Syriacam non quantitatis sed *accentus* tantum rationem habere, versusque suos *syllabarum numero metiri*. Quâ tamen poëseos Syriacæ conditione *varietas morarum in pronuntiandis vocalibus observandarum* non tollitur."]

Moreover, too, the will of the three who were not burned,
   And of him who was burned, is one and the same, in this case and in that;[1]
And, had its Lord commanded the fire to burn them,
   [Even] those three on their part, burned they would have been;
And, if he had signified to it that it should not burn that one man also,
   He would not have been burned; nor had it been of himself that he was rescued.
To go into the fire was of their own will, when they went in;
   But that they were not burned—[because] the Lord of the fire willed and commanded it.
Therefore one equal beauty is that of him who was burned,
   And that of him who was not burned, because the will also was equal.

Beloved martyr! exalted is thy beauty; exalted is thy rank:
   Graceful too thy crown, and mingled thy story with [that of] the glorious.
Choice gold art thou, and the fire hath tried thee, and resplendent is thy beauty.
   And lo! into the King's crown art thou wrought, along with the victorious.
Good workman! who, in the doctrine of the Son of God,
   Pursueth his course like a valiant[2] man, because of the beauty of his faith.

Habib the martyr was a teacher of that which is true;
   A preacher also, whose mouth was full of faith.
Watchful was he, and prompt [for service]; and he encouraged with his teaching
   The household of the house of God, through his faith.
Of light was he full, and he wrestled with the darkness
   Which overspread the country from the paganism which had darkened it.
With the gospel of the Son was his mouth filled in the congregations;
   And as it were a leader of the way did he become to the villages when he arrived in them.

---

[1] [Lit. "here and there."]

[2] [Cureton has "prosperous," which Dr. Payne Smith condemns, remarking: "ܩܪܝܒ I find generally used for the Gk. ἄριστος, and once or twice for κράτιστος. It answers more frequently to *strenuus* = courageous, heroic."]

Zealous he was, because he was concerned for the doctrine
  Divine, that he might establish the adherents[1] of the faith.
At the time when the winds of the pagans blew, a lamp was he,
  And flamed forth whilst they blew upon him, and went not out.
All on fire was he, and filled with the love of his Lord, and was concerned
  For this—that he might speak of him without hindrance.[2]

The thorns of error sprang up in the land from paganism;
  And, as much as in him lay, he rooted them out by his diligence.
He taught, admonished, and confirmed in the faith,
  The friends of Christ,[3] who were harassed by persecutors.
Against sword and against fire did he wrestle,
  With love hot as the flame, and was not afraid.
Like a two-edged brand,[4] keen was
  His faith, and against error did he contend.
Leaven did he prove to be in this land which had become exhausted[5]
  Through fondness for the idols of vanity which error had brought in.
He was like salt by reason of his savoury doctrine
  To this region, which had become insipid through unbelief.

[1] [Lit. "the party" or "side."]

[2] [As in Gal. v. 7, answering to the Gk. ἐγκόπτω. The verb ܩܛܥ (Pa.) properly means to *disquiet* (as in John xiv. 1), then to *hinder*.]

[3] [The ordinary word for "Christians" in these documents is the borrowed Χριστιανοί: here a native word is used, formed from the one which we read as "Messiah."]

[4] [A corruption of the word σαμψηρά is used here. It is said by Josephus, *Antiq.* xx. 2. 3, to have been the name given by the Assyrians to some kind of sword. Suidas mentions it as a barbarian word for σπάθη, a *broadsword*. Cureton's "scimetar" would be preferable, as being somewhat more distinctive, if it appeared that a scimetar could have two edges.]

[5] [The temptation was strong to render ܩܠܒ "became unleavened" (or "tasteless"), a sense apparently required by the decided figure employed and by the language of the next couplet, where "insipid" corresponds to "salt." The word ܩܠܒܐ (= ἄζυμον), moreover, if not the Arabic قلب (to which Schaaf, though it does not appear on what authority, assigns the meaning "*sine fermento* massam subegit"), seems to point in the same direction. Dr. Payne Smith, however, is not aware of any instance of the proposed meaning: he says, "My examples make ܩܠܒ = ἐκλείπω, to fail."]

A deacon was he, and filled the place of a high-priest
　By the preaching and teaching of that which is true.
He was to the flock a good shepherd whilst he was [its] overseer;
　And his life laid he down for the flock while he tended it.
He chased away the wolf, and drove off from it the beast of prey.
　And he repaired the breaches, and gathered the lambs into their folds.
He went out secretly [and] encouraged the congregations:
　He strengthened them, and exhorted them, and held them up.
And he forged armour of faith, and put it on them,
　That they might not be ignominiously overthrown[1] by the paganism which abounded.
The flocks of the fold of the Son of God were being laid waste
　By persecutors: and he encouraged the lambs and the ewes.
And he was an advocate to the household of faith;
　And he taught them not to be daunted by persecutors.
He taught them to run to meet death,
　Without being afraid either of sword or of fire.
In the teaching of the Son of God he prospered,
　So that his faith pursued its course without dread.

Then error grew envious, became furious, and was maddened, because of him;
　And she pursued after him, that she might shed upon the earth innocent blood.
The Defamer, who hates the race of men,
　Laid snares for him, that he might rid the place of his presence.[2]
He who hateth the truth pursued after him to put him to death,
　That he might make his voice to cease[3] from the teaching of the house of God.
And error raised an outcry [demanding] that Habib should die, because she hated him;
　Vexation goaded her on, and she sought to take away his life.

His story was talked about[4] before the pagan judge of the country,
　And the dear fame of him reached the king: who in great rage,
And because the diadem was interwoven with paganism, decreed[5] death
　Against Habib, because he was full of faith.

---

[1] [Or "brought to contempt."]   [2] [Lit. "society."]
[3] [Or "that his voice might cease."]   [4] [Lit. "mooted."]
[5] Lit. "reached the king in great rage (*i.e. so as to cause* great rage, ܠ being often = *ܠ;* denoting result), and, because ..., he decreed."—Dr. PAYNE SMITH.

And, when the command reached the judge, he armed himself
  With rage and fury; and, with a mind thirsting for blood,
And like hunters who lay nets for the young stag,
  After Habib did they go out to catch [him].

But this man was a preacher of the faith,
  Who in the highway of the crucifixion was prospering;
And, that he might benefit by his teaching the children of his people,
  His work embraced the countries round about him.
So, when error went out after him, she found him not:
  Not that he was fled, but that he had gone out to preach the gospel.
Then, because of the fury of the pagans, which was great beyond all that was meet,
  His kindred and his mother did they seize for his sake.

Blessed art thou, O woman! mother since thou art of the martyr.
  For wherefore was it that they seized thee [and] bound thee, iniquitously?
What do they require of thee, O thou full of beauty? What, [I ask], have they required of thee?
  Lo! they require of thee that thou bring the martyr, that he may be a sacrifice.
Bring, oh bring thy sweet fruit to the place of the oblation—
  [The fruit] whose smell is fragrant, that it may be incense to the Godhead.
Fair shoot, thy cluster bring from where it is,
  That its wine may be for a libation whose taste is sweet.

The lamb heard that they were seeking him, that he might be a sacrifice;
  And he set out and came to the sacrificers rejoicing.
He heard that others also were being afflicted for his sake,
  And he came that he might bear the suffering which was his, in the stead of many.
The lot fell on him, to be himself alone a sacrifice;
  And the fire that was to offer him up was looking out [for him] until he came.
Of the many who were bound for his sake
  Not one single person was seized to die, but only he.
He it was that was worthy, and for him was martyrdom reserved;
  And to snatch the martyr's place no man was able.
And therefore of his own will did he present himself
  To the judge, that he might be seized, and die for Jesus' sake.

He heard that they sought him, and he came that he might be
  seized, even as they sought him :
And he went in of himself before the judge, and dauntless was
  his look.
He hid not himself, nor did he wish to flee from the judge :
For with light was he imbued, and from the darkness he would
  not flee.

No robber [was he], no murderer, no thief,
  No child of night : but all his course was run in open day.
Wherefore from his flock should the good shepherd flee,
  And leave his fold to be devoured by robbers ?
Wherefore should the physician flee, who goeth forth to heal
  diseases,
And to cure souls by the blood of the Son of God ?
A fearless countenance [1] did the [brave] man carry with him, and
  a great heart ;
And to meet death he ran, rejoicing, for Jesus' sake.

He went in, he stood before the judge, saying to him :
  I am Habib, whom ye sought : lo ! [here] I stand.
And the pagan trembled, and amazement seized him, and he mar-
  velled at him—
At the man who was not afraid, either of sword or of fire.
While he thought that he was fleeing apace, he entered in and
  mocked him ;
And the judge shook, for he saw him courageous in the [very]
  face of death.

A disciple he of that Son of God who said :
  "Rise, come, let us go : for he that betrayeth me lo ! is here."
And to the crucifiers, again, He said : "Whom seek ye ?"
  They say : "Jesus." And He said to them : "I am He."
The Son of God of His own will came to the cross ;
  And on Him the martyr looked, and presented himself [uncom-
  pelled] before the judge.

And the pagan beheld him, and was smitten with fear, and was
  exasperated [against him].
His rage was excited, and he began in his fury to put to him
  questions.[2]

---

[1] [Lit. "openness of countenance."]
[2] [Prop. "agitate questions."]

And, as if he had been one who had shed on the ground the blood of the slain,
 He proceeded to question the saintly man, but he was not ashamed:
Menacing him, and trying to terrify him, and to frighten him,
 And recounting the sufferings which were being prepared by him on his account.

But Habib, when questioned, was not afraid,
 Was not ashamed, and was not frightened by the menaces [he heard].
Lifting up his voice, he confessed Jesus, the Son of God—
 That he was His servant, and was His priest, and His minister.[1]
At the fury of the pagans, roaring at him like lions,
 He trembled not, nor ceased[2] from the confession of the Son of God.
He was scourged, and the scourgings were very dear to him,
 Seeing that he bore a little of the stripes of the Son of God.
He was put into bonds,[3] and he looked on his Lord, whom also they had bound;
 And his heart rejoiced that in the path of His sufferings he had begun to walk.
He ascended the block,[4] and they tore him with combs, but his soul was radiant with light,
 Because he was [deemed] worthy that on him should come the agony of the sufferings of crucifixion.

In the pathway of death had he set his face to walk,
 And what could he desire to find in it but sufferings?
The fire of sacrifice[5] was betrothed to him, and for her did he look;
 And she [on her part] sent him combs, and stripes, and pains, to taste.
All the while that she was coming, she sent him sufferings, that by means of them
 He might be prepared, so that when she met him she might not dismay him.
Sufferings purged him, so that, when the blazing fire should put him to the proof,
 There might not be any dross [found] in his choice gold.
And he endured the whole of the pains that came upon him,
 That he might have experience [of suffering], and in the burning stand like a brave man.

---

[1] [Or "deacon."]   [2] [Or "so as to cease."]
[3] [Lit. "he entered into bondage."]   [4] [The *equuleus* is meant.]
[5] [Or "of the sacrifices."]

And he accepted rejoicing the sufferings which he had to bear:
  For he knew that at their termination he should find death.
And he was not afraid, either of death or of sufferings:
  For with that wine of the crucifixion his heart was drunk.
He despised his body, while it was being dragged along by the persecutors;
  And his limbs, while they were being torn asunder in bitter agony.[1]
Scourges on his back, combs on his sides, stocks on his feet,
  And fire in front of him: still was he brave and full of faith.

They taunted him: Lo! thou worshippest a man;
  But he said: A man I worship not,
But God, who took a body and became man:
  Him do I worship, because He is God with Him that begat Him.
The faith of Habib, the martyr, was full of light;
  And by it was enlightened Edessa, the faithful [city].
The daughter of Abgar, whom Addæus betrothed to the crucifixion—
  Through it is her light, through it her truth and her faith.
Her king is from it, her martyrs from it, her truth from it;
  The teachers also of [her] faith are from it.
Abgar believed that Thou art God, the Son of God;
  And he received a blessing because of the beauty of his faith.
Sharbil the martyr, son of the Edessæans, moreover said:
  My heart is led captive by God, who became man.
And Habib the martyr, who also was crowned at Edessa,
  Confessed these things: that he took a body and became man;
That He is the Son of God, and also is God, and became man.
Edessa learned from teachers the things that are true:
  Her king taught her, her martyrs taught her, the faith;
  But to others, who were fraudulent teachers, she would not hearken.
Habib the martyr, in the ear of Edessa, thus cried aloud
  Out of the midst of the fire: A man I worship not,
But God, who took a body and became man—
  Him do I worship. [Thus] confessed the martyr with uplifted voice.
From confessors torn with combs, burnt, raised up [on the block], slain,
  And [from] a righteous king, did Edessa learn the faith,
And she knows our Lord—that He is even God, the Son of God;
  She also learned and firmly believed that He took a body and became man.

[1] [Lit. "bitterly."]

Not from common scribes did she learn the faith:
> Her king taught her, her martyrs taught her; and she firmly believed them:

And, if she be calumniated as having ever worshipped a man,
> She points to her martyrs, who died for Him as being God.

A man I worship not, said Habib,
> Because it is written: "Cursed is he that putteth his trust in a man."[1]

Forasmuch as He is God, I worship Him, yea submit to be burned
> For His sake, nor will I renounce His faith.

This truth has Edessa held fast from her youth,
> And in her old age she will not barter it away as a daughter of the poor.

Her righteous king became to her a scribe, and from him she learned
> Concerning our Lord—that He is the Son of God, yea God.

Addæus, who brought the bridegroom's ring and put it on her hand,
> Betrothed her thus to the Son of God, who is the Only[-begotten].

Sharbil the priest, who made trial and proof of all gods,
> Died, even as he said, "for God who became man."

Shamuna and Guria, for the sake of the Only[-begotten],
> Stretched out their necks [to receive the stroke], and for Him died, forasmuch as He is God.

And Habib the martyr, who was teacher of congregations,
> Preached of Him, that He took a body and became man.

For a man the martyr would not have [submitted to be] burned in the fire;
> But he was burned "for the sake of God who became man."

And Edessa is witness that thus he confessed while he was being burned:
> And from the confession of a martyr that has been burned who is he that can escape?

All minds does faith reduce to silence and despise—
> [She] that is full of light and stoopeth not to shadows.

She despiseth him that maligns the Son by denying that He is God;
> Him too that saith "He took not a body and became man."

In faith which was full of truth he stood upon the fire;
> And he became incense, and propitiated with his fragrance the Son of God.

In all [his] afflictions, and in all [his] tortures, and in all [his] sufferings,
> Thus did he confess, and thus did he teach the blessed [city].

---

[1] [Jer. xvii. 5.]

And this truth did Edessa hold fast touching our Lord—
  Even that He is God, and of Mary became a man.
And the bride hates him that denies His Godhead,
  And despises and contemns him that maligns His corporeal nature.
And she recognises Him [as] One in Godhead and in manhood—
  The Only[-begotten], whose body is inseparable from Him.
And thus did the daughter of the Parthians learn to believe,
  And thus did she firmly hold, and thus does she teach him that listens to her.

The judge, therefore, full of [zeal for] paganism, commanded
  That the martyr should be led forth and burned in the fire which was reserved for him.
And forthwith a strap was thrust into his mouth, as [though he had been] a murderer,
  His confession being kept within his heart towards God.
And they hurried him away, and he went out from the judgment-hall, rejoicing
  That the hour was come when the crown should be given to his faith.
And there went out with him crowds of people, that they might bear him company,
  Looking upon him, not as a dead man accompanied [to his burial],
But as a man who was going away that by means of fire he might become a bridegroom,
  And that there might be bestowed the crown which was by righteousness reserved for him.
They looked upon him as upon a man entering into battle,
  And around him were spears, and lances, and swords, but he vanquished them.
They beheld him going up like a champion from the contest,
  And in his triumph chaplets were brought to him by those who beheld.
They looked upon him as he vanquished principalities and powers,
  Which all made war with him, and he put them to shame.
The whole congregation of the followers of Christ exulted over him,
  Because he raised up the friends [1] of the faith by the sufferings which he bore.
There went forth with him the church, a bride full of light;
  And her face was beaming on the beloved martyr who was united to her.
Then did his mother, because it was the marriage-feast for her son,
  Deck herself in garments nobler than her wont.

[1] [Lit. "side," or "party."]

Since sordid raiment suited not the banquet-hall,
   In magnificent [attire] all white she clad herself right tastefully.
Hither to the battle came down love to fight
   In the mother's soul—[the love] of nature, and [the love] of God.
She looked upon her son as he went forth to be put into the flame;
   And, forasmuch as there was in her the love of the Lord, she suffered not.
The yearnings of her mother's womb cried out on behalf of its fruit;
   But faith silenced them, so that their tumult ceased.
Nature shrieked over the limb which was severed from her;
   But the love of the Lord intoxicated the soul, that she should not perceive it.
Nature loved, but the love of the Lord did conquer in the strife
   Within the soul of the mother, that she should not grieve for her beloved.
And, instead of suffering, her heart was filled with all emotions of joy;
   And, instead of mourning, she went forth in splendid apparel.
And she accompanied him as he went out to be burned, and was elate,
   Because the love of the Lord vanquished that of nature.
And [clad] in white, as for a bridegroom, she made a marriage-feast—
   [She] the mother of the martyr, and was blithe because of him.
"Shamuna the Second" may we call this blessed [one]:
   Since, had seven been burned instead of one, she had been well content.
One she had, and she gave him to be food for the fire;
   And, even as that one, if she had had seven, she had given [them all].
He was cast into the fire, and the blaze kindled around him;
   And his mother looked on, and grieved not at his burning.
Another eye, which gazeth upon the things unseen,
   Was in her soul, and by reason of this she exulted when he was being burned.
On the gems of light which are in martyrs' crowns she looked,
   And on the glory which is laid up for them after their sufferings;
And [on] the promised blessings which they inherit yonder through their afflictions,
   And [on] the Son of God who clothes their limbs with light;
And [on] the manifold beauties of that kingdom which shall not be dissolved,
   And [on] the ample door which is opened for them to enter in to God.

On these did the martyr's mother look when he was being burned,
  And she rejoiced, she exulted, and in white did she go forth
    with him.
She looked upon him while the fire consumed his frame,
  And, forasmuch as his crown was very noble, she grieved not.

The sweet root was thrown into the fire, upon the coals;
  And it turned to incense, and cleansed the air from pollution.
With the fumes of sacrifice had the air been polluted,
  And by the burning of this martyr was it cleansed.
The firmament was fetid with the exhalations from [1] the altars;
  And there rose up the sweet perfume of the martyr, and it grew
    sweet thereby.
And the sacrifices ceased, and there was peace in the assemblies;
  And the sword was blunted, that it should no more lay waste
    the friends of Christ.
With Sharbil it began, with Habib it ended, in our land;
  And from that time [2] even until now not one has it slain, since
    he was burned.
Constantine, chief of conquerors, took the empire,
  And the cross has trampled on the diadem of the emperor, and
    is set upon his head.
Broken is the lofty horn of idolatry,
  And from the burning of the martyr even until now not one has
    it pierced.
His smoke arose, and it became incense to the Godhead;
  And by it was the air purged which was tainted by paganism,
  And by his burning was the whole land cleansed:
    Blessed be he that gave him a crown, and glory, and a good name!

[Here] endeth the Homily on Habib the martyr, composed by Mar Jacob.

A HOMILY ON GURIA AND SHAMUNA, COMPOSED BY MAR JACOB.

Shamuna and Guria, martyrs who made themselves illustrious in
    their afflictions,
  Have in love required of me to tell of their illustrious deeds.
To champions of the faith the doctrine calleth me,
  That I should go and behold their contests and their crowns.

[1] [Lit. "the sacrifices of."]   [2] [Lit. "from him."]

Children of the right hand, who have done battle against the left,
  Have called me this day to recite the marvellous tale of their
    conflicts :—
Simple old men, who entered into the fight like heroes,
  And nobly distinguished themselves in the strife of blood:
Those who were the salt of our land, and it was sweetened thereby,
  And its savour was restored, which had become insipid through
    unbelief:
Candlesticks of gold, which were full of the oil of the crucifixion,
  By which was lighted up all our region, which had turned to
    darkness:
Two lamps, of which, when all the winds were blowing
  Of every [kind of] error, the lights were not put out:
Good labourers, who from the spring of day laboured
  In the blessed vineyard of the house of God right duteously:
Bulwarks of our land, who became to us as it were a defence
  Against all spoilers in all the wars that surrounded us:
Havens of peace, a place also of retreat for all that were distressed,
  And a resting-place for the head of every one that was in need
    of succour:
Two precious pearls, which were
  An ornament for the bride of my lord Abgar, the Aramæan's
    son.

Teachers they were who practised their teaching in blood,
  And whose faith was known by their sufferings.
On their bodies they wrote the story of the Son of God
  With [the marks of] combs and scourges which thickly covered
    them.
They showed their love, not by words of the mouth alone,
  But by tortures and by the rending of their limbs asunder.
For the love of the Son of God they gave up their bodies:
  Since it beseemeth the lover that for his love he should give up
    himself.
Fire and sword proved their love, how true [it was];
  And more beautiful than silver tried in [a furnace of] earth
    were their necks.

They looked on God, and, because they saw His exalted beauties,
  Therefore did they look with contempt upon their sufferings for
    His sake.
The Sun of righteousness had arisen in their hearts;
  And they were enlightened by it, and with [His] light chased
    they away the darkness.

At the idols of vanity, which error had brought in, they laughed,
  Instinct with the faith of the Son of God which is full of light.
The love of the Lord was as a fire in their hearts;
  Nor could all the brambles of idolatry stand before it.
Fixed was their love on God unchangeably:[1]
  And therefore did they look with scorn upon the sword,[2] all athirst as it was for blood.

With guilelessness and [yet with] wisdom stood they in the judgment-hall,
  As they had been commanded by the Teacher of that which is true.
Despising as they did kindred and family, guileless were they;
  Forasmuch, also, as possessions and wealth were held in no account by them.
[Nor guileless only]: for in the judgment-hall with the wisdom of serpents [too]
  They were heedful of the faith of the house of God.

When a serpent is seized and struck, he guards his head,
  But gives up and leaves exposed all his body to his captors:
And, so long as his head is kept [from harm], his life abideth in him;
  But, if the head be struck, his life is left [a prey] to destruction.
The head of the soul is men's faith;
  And, if this be preserved [unharmed], by it is also preserved their life:[3]
Even though the whole body be lacerated with blows,
  [Yet], so long as faith is preserved, the soul is alive;
But, if faith is struck [down] by unbelief,
  Lost is the soul, and life has perished from the man.

Shamuna and Guria of the faith as men[4]
  Were heedful, that it should not be struck [down] by persecutors:
For they knew that, if faith is preserved,
  Both soul and body are preserved from destruction.
And, because of this, touching their faith were they solicitous,
  That that should not be struck [down] in which their very life was hidden.

---

[1] [Or "who changes not."]   [2] [Σαμψηρά.]
[3] [Or "salvation:" a different word from that used in speaking of the serpent.]
[4] [Lit. "as a man."]

They gave up their bodies both to blows and to dislocation,[1]
 Yea to every [kind of] torture, that their faith should not be
  stricken [down];
And, even as the serpent also hides his head from blows,
 So hid they their faith within their hearts;
And the body was smitten, and endured stripes, and bore sufferings:
 But overthrown was not their faith which was within their hearts.

The mouth betrayeth the soul to death when it speaks,
 And with the tongue, as with a sword, worketh slaughter.
And from it spring up both life and death to men:
 Denying [a man] dies, confessing he lives, and [the mouth] hath
  power over it.
Denial is death, and in confession is the soul's life;
 And power hath the mouth over them both, like a judge.
The word of the mouth openeth the door for death to enter in;
 This, too, calleth for life, and it beameth forth upon the man.
Even the robber by one word of faith
 Won him the kingdom, and became heir of paradise,[2] all fraught
  with blessings.
The wicked judges too, from the martyrs, the sons of the right
 hand,
Demanded that by word of mouth only they should blaspheme;
But, like true men holding fast the faith,
 They uttered not a word by which unbelief might be served.

Shamuna, beauty of our faith, who is adequate to [tell of] thee?
 All too narrow is my mouth for thy praise, too mean for thee
  to be spoken of by it.
Thy truth is thy beauty, thy crown thy suffering, thy wealth thy
 stripes,
 And by reason of thy blows magnificent is the beauty of thy
  championship.
Proud of thee is our country, as of a treasury which is full of gold:
 Since wealth art thou to us, and a coveted store which cannot
  be stolen [from us].

Guria, martyr, staunch hero of our faith,
 Who shall suffice thee, to recount thy beauties divine?
Lo! tortures on thy body are set like gems of beryl,
 And the sword on thy neck like a chain of choice gold.
Thy blood upon thy form is a robe of glory full of beauty,
 And the scourging of thy back a vesture with which the sun
  may not compare.

---

[1] [Or "rending asunder."]   [2] [Lit. "the garden.]

Radiant thou art and comely by virtue of these thy sufferings, so
    abounding;
  And resplendent are thy beauties, because of the pains which
    are [so] severe upon thee.
Shamuna, our riches, richer art thou than the rich:
  For lo! the rich stand at thy door, that thou mayest relieve them.
Small thy village, poor thy country: who, then, gave thee
  That lords of villages and cities should court thy favour?
Lo! judges in their robes and vestments
  Take dust from thy threshold, as [though it were] the medicine
    of life.
The cross is rich, and to its worshippers increaseth riches;
  And its poverty despiseth all the riches of the world.

Shamuna and Guria, sons of the poor, lo! at your doors
  Bow down the rich, that they may receive from you [supplies
    for] their wants.
The Son of God in poverty and want
  Showed to the world that all its riches are as nothing.
[His disciples], all fishermen, all poor, all weak,
  All men of little note, became illustrious through His faith.
One fisherman, whose *village* too was a home of fishermen,[1]
  He made chief over the twelve, yea head of the house.[2]
One a tentmaker, who aforetime was a persecutor,
  He seized upon, and made him a chosen vessel for the faith.

Shamuna and Guria came from villages that were not wealthy,
  And lo! in a great city became they lords;
And its chief men, its judges also, stand before their doors,
  And they solicit their charity to satisfy their wants.
From their confession of the faith of the Son of God
  These blessed men acquired riches beyond compute.
Poor did He Himself become, and the poor made He rich;
  And lo! enriched is the whole creation through His poverty.

The chosen martyrs did battle against error,
  And in the confession of the Son of God stood they firm like
    valiant men.
They went in and confessed Him before the judge with look un-
    daunted,[3]
  That He too might confess them, even as they confessed Him,
    before His Father.

---

[1] [*i.e.* "Bethsaida."]   [2] [Or "steward."]
[3] [Lit. "with openness of countenance."]

There arose against them the war of pagans like a tempest;
  But the cross was their helmsman, and steered them on.
They were required to sacrifice to lifeless images,
  But they departed not from their confession of the Son of God.
The wind of idolatry blew in their faces,
  But they themselves were as rocks piled up against the hurricane.
Like a swift whirlwind, error snatched at them;
  But, forasmuch as they were sheltered by the crucifixion, it hurt them not.
The Evil One set on all his dogs to bark, that they might bite them;
  But, forasmuch as they had the cross for a staff, they put them all to flight.

But who is sufficient to tell of their contests,
  Or their sufferings, or the rending asunder of their limbs?
Or who can paint the picture of their coronation,[1]
  How they went up from the contest covered with glory?
To judgment they went in, but of the judge they took no account;
  Nor were they anxious what they should say when questioned.
The judge menaced [them], and multiplied his words of threatening;
  And recounted tortures and all [kinds of] inflictions, that he might terrify them.
He spake great words,[2] that by fright and intimidation,
  By menaces too, he might incline them to sacrifice.
Yet the combatants despised the menaces, and the intimidations,
  And the sentence of judgment, and all bodily deaths;
And they prepared themselves for insult and stripes, and for blows,
  And for provocation, and to be dragged along, and to be burnt;
For imprisonment also, and for bonds, and for all evil things,
  And for all tortures, and for all sufferings, rejoicing all the while.
They were not alarmed nor affrighted, nor dismayed,
  Nor did the sharpness of the tortures bend them to sacrifice.
Their body they despised, and as dung upon the ground accounted they it:
  For they knew that, the more it was beaten, the more would its beauty increase;
And, the more the judge increased his menaces to alarm them,
  The more did they show their contempt of him, having no fear of his threats.
He kept telling them what tortures he had prepared for them;
  And they continued telling him about Gehenna, which was reserved for him.

---

[1] [Lit. "portray the image of their crowns."]
[2] [Lit. "magnified his words."]

By those things which he told [them] he tried to frighten them to
    sacrifice;
And they spoke to him about the fearful judgment yonder.
Truth is wiser than wise words,
    And very hateful, however much it may be adorned, is falsehood.
Shamuna and Guria went on speaking truth,
    While the judge continued to utter falsehood.
And therefore were they not afraid of his threatening,
    Because all his menaces against the truth were accounted [by
        them] as empty sound.[1]

The intercourse of the world they despised, they contemned and
        scorned, [yea] they abandoned;
    And to return to it they had no wish, or to enter it [again].
From the place of judgment they set their faces to depart
    To that meeting-place for them all, the life of the new world.
They cared neither for possessions nor for houses,
    Nor for the advantages of this world, so full of evil.
In the world of light was their heart bound captive with God,
    And to *that* country did they set their face to depart;
And they looked to the sword, to come and be a bridge
    To let them pass over to God, for whom they were longing.
This world they accounted as a little tent,
    But that yonder as a city full of beauties;
And they were in haste by the sword to depart hence
    To the land of light, which is full of blessing for those who are
        worthy of it.

The judge commanded to hang them up by their arms,
    And without mercy did they stretch them out in bitter agony.
A demon's fury breathed rage into the heart of the judge,
    And embittered him against the stedfast ones, [inciting him]
        to crush them;
And between the height and the depth he stretched them out to
        afflict them:
    And they were a marvel to both sides, [when they saw] how
        much they endured.
At the old men's frame heaven and earth marvelled,
    [To see] how much suffering it bore nor cried out for help
        under [their] affliction.
Hung up and dragged along are their feeble bodies by their arms,
    Yet is there deep silence, nor is there one that cries out for help
        or that murmurs.

[1] [Lit. " as breath."]

Amazed were all who beheld their contests,
  [To see] how [calmly] the outstretched forms bore the inflictions
    [laid upon them].[1]
Amazed too was Satan at their spotless frames,
  [To see] what weight of affliction they sustained without a groan.
Yea, and gladdened too were the angels by that fortitude [of
    theirs],
  [To see] how patiently it bore that contest [so] terrible that was.
But, as combatants who were awaiting their crowns,
  There entered no sense of weariness into their minds.
Nay, it was the judge that grew weary; yea, he was astonished:
  But the noble men [before him] felt no weariness in their
    afflictions.

He asked them whether they would consent to sacrifice;
  But the mouth was unable to speak from pain.
Thus did the persecutors increase their inflictions,
  Until they gave no place for the word to be spoken.
Silent was the mouth from the inflictions laid on their limbs;
  But the will, like that of a hero, was nerved with fortitude from
    itself.
Alas for the persecutors! how destitute were they of righteousness!
  But the children of light—how were they clad in faith!
They demand speech, when there is no place for speaking,
  Since the word of the mouth was forbidden them by pain.
Fast bound was the body, and silent the mouth, and it was unable
  To utter the word when unrighteously questioned.

And what should the martyr do, who had no power to say,
  When he was questioned, that he would not sacrifice?
All silent were the old men full of faith,
  And from pain they were incapable of speaking.
Yet questioned they were: and in what way, if a man is silent
  When he is questioned, shall he assent to that which is said?
But the old men, that they might not be thought to assent,
  Expressed clearly by signs the word which it behoved them to
    speak.
Their heads they shook, and, instead of speech, by a dumb sign
    they showed
  The resolve of the new man that was within.
Their heads hung down, signifying amidst their pains
  That they were not going to sacrifice, and every one understood
    their meaning.

[1] [Lit. "how much the outstretched forms bore in consequence of the inflictions."]

As long as there was in them place for speech, with speech did
    they confess;
But, when it was forbidden them by pain, they spake with a
    dumb sign.
Of faith they spoke both with the voice and without the voice:
    So that, when speaking and also when silent, they were [alike]
    stedfast.

Who but must be amazed at the path of life, how narrow it is,
    And how straight to him that desires to walk in it?
Who but must marvel [to see] that, when the will is watchful and
    ready,
    It is very broad and full of light to him that goeth therein?
About the path are ditches; full also is it of pitfalls;
    And, if one turn but a little aside from it, a ditch receives him.
That dumb sign only is there between the right and the left,
    And on *Yea* and *Nay* stand[1] sin and righteousness.
By a dumb sign only did the blessed men plainly signify that they
    would not sacrifice,
    And in virtue of a single dumb sign did the path lead them to Eden;
And, if this same dumb sign had inclined and turned down but a
    little
    Toward the depth, the path of the old men would have been to
    Gehenna.
Upwards they made a sign, [to signify] that upwards were they
    prepared to ascend;
    And in consequence of that sign they ascended and mingled
    with the heavenly ones.
Between sign and sign were Paradise and Gehenna:
    They made a sign that they would not sacrifice, and they in-
    herited the place of the kingdom.

Even while they were silent they were advocates for the Son of God:
    For not in multitude of words doth faith consist.
That fortitude of theirs was a full-voiced confession,
    And as though with open mouth declared they [their] faith by
    signs;
And every one knew what they were saying, though silent,
    And enriched and increased was the faith of the house of God;
And error was put to shame by reason of two old men, who,
    though they spake not,
    Vanquished it; and they kept silence, and their faith stood fast.
And, though tempestuous accents were heard from the judge,
    And the commands of the emperor were dreadful, yea violent,

---

[1] [Or "depend."]

And paganism had a bold face and an open mouth,
  And its voice was raised, and silent were the old men with pain,
[Yet] null and void became the command and drowned was the
    voice of the judge,
  And without speech the mute sign of the martyrs bore off the palm.
Talking and clamour, and the sound of stripes, on the left;
  And deep silence and suffering standing on the right;
And, by one mute sign with which the old men pointed above
    their heads,
  The head of faith was lifted up, and error was put to shame.
Worsted in the encounter were they who spoke, and the victory
    was to the silent:
  For, voiceless they uttered by signs the discourse of faith.

They took them down, because they had vanquished while silent;
  And they put them in bonds, threatening [yet] to vanquish them.
Bonds and a dungeon void of light were by the martyrs
    Held of no account—yea [rather] as the light which has no end.
[To be] without bread, and without water, and without light,
  Pleased them well, because of the love of the Son of God.

The judge commanded by their feet to hang them up
  With their heads downwards, by a sentence all unrighteous:
Hanged up was Shamuna with his head downwards; and he prayed
  [In] prayer pure and strained clear by pain.
Sweet fruit was hanging on the tree in that judgment-hall,
  And its taste and smell made the very denizens of heaven to marvel.
Afflicted was his body, but sound was his faith;
  Bound fast was his person, but unfettered was his prayer over
    his deed.
For, prayer nothing whatsoever turneth aside,
  And [nothing] hindereth it—not even sword, not even fire.
His form was turned upside down, but [his] prayer was unrestrained,
  And straight was its path on high to the abode of the angels.
The more the affliction of the chosen martyr was increased,
  The more from his lips was all confession heard.
The martyrs longed for the whetted sword affectionately,
  And sought it as a treasure full of riches.

A new work has the Son of God wrought in the world—
  That dreadful death should be yearned for [1] by many.
That men should run to meet the sword is a thing unheard of,
  Except they were those whom Jesus has enlisted in His service
    by His crucifixion.

[1] [Or "beloved."]

That death is bitter, every one knoweth lo! from earliest time :
To martyrs alone is it not bitter to be slain.
They laughed at the whetted sword when they saw it,
And greeted it with smiles: for it was that which was the occasion of their crowns.
As though it had been something hated, they left the body to be beaten:
Even though loving it, they held it not back from pains.
For the sword they waited, and the sword went forth and crowned them :
Because for it they looked; and it came to meet them, even as they desired.
The Son of God slew death by His crucifixion ;
And, inasmuch as death is slain, it caused no suffering to the martyrs.

With a wounded serpent one playeth without fear ;
A slain lion even a coward will drag along :
The great serpent our Lord crushed by His crucifixion ;
The dread lion did the Son of God slay by His sufferings.
Death bound He fast, and laid him prostrate and trampled on him at the gate of Hades ;
And [now] whosoever will draweth near and mocketh at him, because he is slain.
These old men, Shamuna and Guria, mocked at death,
As at that lion which by the Son of God was slain.
The great serpent, which slew Adam among the trees,
Who could seize, so long as he drank not of the blood of the cross ?
The Son of God crushed the dragon by His crucifixion,
And lo! boys and old men mock at the wounded serpent.
Pierced is the lion with the spear which [pierced] the side of the Son of God;
And whosoever will trampleth on him, and despiseth him, yea mocketh at him.

The Son of God—He is the cause of all good things,
And Him doth it behove every mouth to celebrate.
He did Himself espouse [1] the bride with the blood which flowed from His wounds,
And of His wedding-friends He demanded as a nuptial gift [2] the blood of their necks.

[1] [Lit. "purchase."]

[2] ܒܠܘܥܣ, though not in the lexicons, is the same word that appears in Castel as ܒܠܘܥܣܐ.

The Lord of the wedding-feast hung on the cross in nakedness,
    And whosoever came to be a guest, He let fall His blood upon
        him.
Shamuna and Guria gave up their bodies for His sake
    To sufferings and tortures and to all the various forms of woe.[1]
At Him they looked as He was mocked by wicked men,
    And thus did they themselves endure mockery without a groan.

Edessa was enriched by your slaughter, O blessed ones:
    For ye adorned her with your crowns and with your sufferings.
Her beauty are ye, her bulwark ye, her salt ye,
    Her riches and her store, yea her boast and all her treasure.
Faithful stewards are ye:[2]
    Since by your sufferings ye did array the bride in beauty.
The daughter of the Parthians, who was espoused to the cross,[3]
    Of *you* maketh her boast: since by your teaching lo! she was
        enlightened.
Her advocates are ye; scribes who, though silent, vanquished
    All error, whilst its voice was uplifted high in unbelief.

Those old men[4] of the daughter of the Hebrews were sons of Belial,[5]
False witnesses, who killed Naboth, feigning themselves [to be
        true].
Her did Edessa outdo by her two old men full of beauty,
    Who were witnesses to the Son of God, and died like Naboth.
Two were there, and two here, old men;
    And these were called witnesses, and witnesses those.
Let us now see which of them were witnesses chosen of God,
    And which city is beloved by reason of her old men and of her
        honourable ones.
Lo! the sons of Belial who slew Naboth are witnesses;
    And here Shamuna and Guria, again, are witnesses.
Let us now see which witnesses, and which old men,
    And which city can stand with confidence[6] before God.

---

[1] [Lit. "to the forms ($\sigma\chi\acute{\eta}\mu\alpha\tau\alpha$) of all afflictions."]

[2] [This seems preferable to Cureton's "Ye are the stewards of (her) faith." The expression exactly corresponds in form to that in Luke xvi. 8 (Peshito): "the steward of injustice" = "the unjust steward."]

[3] [Lit. "crucifixion."]   [4] [Or "elders."]

[5] [By this name the men referred to (not, however, the elders, but the two false witnesses suborned by them) are called in 1 Kings xxi. 10, 13. The expression in the text is literally "sons of iniquity," and is that used by the Peshito.]

[6] [Or "have an open countenance."]

Sons of Belial were those witnesses of that adulterous woman,
   And lo! their shame is all portrayed in their names.
Edessa's just and righteous old men, her witnesses,
   Were like Naboth, who himself also was slain for righteousness' sake.
They were not like the two lying sons of Belial,
   Nor is Edessa like Zion, which also crucified [the Lord].
Like herself her old men were false, yea dared
   To shed on the ground innocent blood wickedly.
[But] by these witnesses here lo! the truth is spoken.—
   Blessed be He who gave us the treasure-store of their crowns!

[Here] endeth the Homily on Guria and Shamuna.

A CANTICLE OF MAR[1] JACOB THE TEACHER ON EDESSA, WHEN SHE SENT TO [REQUEST] OUR LORD TO COME TO HER.[2]

Edessa sent to Christ by an epistle to come to her and enlighten her. On behalf of all the peoples did she make intercession to Him that He would leave Zion, which hated Him, and come to the [other] peoples, who loved Him.

She despatched a messenger to Him, and begged of Him to enter into friendship with her. By the righteous king she made intercession to Him, that He would depart from the [one] people, and towards the [other] peoples direct His burden.

From among all kings one wise king did the daughter of the peoples find. Ambassador she made him. To her Lord she sent by him: Come Thou unto me; I will forget in Thee all idols and carved images.

The harlot heard the report of Him from afar, as she was standing in the street, going astray with idols, playing the wench with carved images. She loved, she much desired Him, when He was far away, and begged Him to admit her into His chamber.

---

[1] [Or "My Lord," or "Mr."]
[2] This is taken from Cod. Add. 17,158, fol. 56.

Let the much-desired Bridegroom kiss me: with the kisses of His mouth let me be blessed. I have heard of Him from afar: may I see Him near; and may I place my lips upon His, and be delighted by seeing Him with mine eyes.

Thy breasts are better to me than wine: for the fragrance of Thy sweetness is life for evermore. With Thy milk shall I be nourished; with Thy fragrance shall I grow sweet from the smoke of idols, which with its rank odour did make me fetid.

Draw me after Thee into Thy fold: for I am a sheep gone astray in the world. After Thee do I run, and Thy converse do I seek: that in me may be completed that number of a hundred, by means of a lost one which is found.

Let Gabriel rejoice and be exceeding glad, with the company of all the angels, in Thee, the Good Shepherd, who on Thy shoulders didst carry the maimed sheep, that that number of a hundred might be preserved.

Thy love is better than wine; than the face of the upright Thy affection. By wine let us be reminded of Thee, how by the cup of Thy blood Thou didst grant us to obtain new life, and the upright did celebrate Thy love.

A church am I from among the peoples, and I have loved the Only-begotten who was sent [by God]: whereas His betrothed hated Him, I have loved Him; and by the hands of Abgar the Black[1] do I beseech Him to come to me and visit me.

Black am I, yet comely. Ye daughters of Zion, blameless is your envy, seeing that the Son of the Glorious One hath espoused me, to bring me into His chamber. Even when I was hateful [to see], He loved me, for He is able to make me fairer than water.

Black was I in sins, but I am comely: for I have repented and turned me. I have put away in baptism that hateful hue, for He hath washed me in His innocent blood who is the Saviour of all creatures.

[Here] end the Extracts from the Canticle on Edessa.

[1] See note on p. 7.

EXTRACTS FROM VARIOUS BOOKS CONCERNING ABGAR THE KING AND ADDÆUS THE APOSTLE.

I.[1]

Of the blessed Addæus the apostle. From his Teaching which he gave in Edessa before Abgar the king and the assembly of the city.

And, when he had entered the sepulchre, he was raised to life again, and came forth from the sepulchre with many [others]. And those who were guarding the sepulchre saw not how He came forth from the sepulchre; but the watchers from on high—they were the proclaimers and announcers of His resurrection. For, had He not [so] willed, He had not died, because He is Lord of death, the exit [from the world]; nor, had it not pleased Him, would He have put on a body, inasmuch as He is Himself the framer of the body. For that will which led Him to stoop to be born of the Virgin, likewise caused Him further to descend to the suffering of death.—*And a little after* [*we read*]: For, although His appearance was that of men, yet His power, and His knowledge, and His authority, were those of God.

II.[2]

From the Teaching of Addæus the apostle, which was spoken in the city of Edessa.

Ye know that I said unto you, that none of the souls which go forth out of the bodies of men are under [the power of] death, but that they all live and continue to exist, and that there are for them mansions and an abode of rest. For the reasoning [power] of the soul does not cease, nor the knowledge, because it is the image of the immortal God. For it is not without perceptions, after the manner of the bodily frame, which has no perception of that corruption which has acquired dominion over it. Recompense, however, and reward it will not receive apart from its bodily form,

---
[1] Taken from Cod. Add. 14,535, fol. i.
[2] From Cod. Add. 12,155, fol. 53 vers.

because what it experiences belongs not to itself alone, but to the bodily form also in which it dwelt for a time. But the disobedient, who have not known God, will then repent without avail.

III.[1]

From the Epistle of Addæus the apostle, which he spake in the city of Edessa.

Give heed to this ministry which ye hold, and with fear and trembling continue ye in it, and minister every day. Minister ye not in it with neglectful habits, but with the discreetness of faith. And let not the praises of Christ cease out of your mouth, and let not any sense of weariness come over you at the season of prayers. Give heed to the verity which ye hold, and to the teaching of the truth which ye have received, and to the teaching of salvation which I commit to you. Because before the tribunal of Christ will it be required of you, when He maketh reckoning with the pastors and overseers, and when He shall take His money from the traders with the usury of what they have taught.[2] For He is the Son of a King, and goeth to receive a kingdom, and He will return and come and make a resuscitation to life of all men.

IV.[3]

Addæus preached at Edessa and in Mesopotamia (he was from Paneus[4]) in the days of Abgar the king. And, when he was among the Zophenians, Severus the son of Abgar sent and slew him at Agel Hasna, as also a young man his disciple.

V.[3]

71. and Narcissus. For they did not suffer that selection of the Seventy-two to be wanting, as likewise neither that of the Twelve. This [man] was [one] of the Seventy-two: perhaps he was a disciple of Addæus the apostle.

---

[1] From Cod. Add. 17,193, fol. 36. [See p. 30.]

[2] [Or " of the doctrines."]

[3] Extracts IV. and V. are from Cod. Add. 14,601, fol. 164, written apparently in the eighth century.

[4] [*i.e.* Paneas.]

VI.[1]

From the Departure of Marath[2] Mary from the World, and the Birth and Childhood of our Lord Jesus Christ. Book the Second.

In the year three hundred and forty-five, in the month of the latter Tishrin,[3] Marath Mary went out from her house, and went to the sepulchre of Christ: because every day she used to go and weep there. But the Jews immediately after the death of Christ seized the sepulchre, and heaped great stones at the door of it. And over the sepulchre and Golgotha they set guards, and commanded them that, if any one should go and pray at the sepulchre or at Golgotha, he should immediately be put to death. And the Jews took away the cross of our Lord, and those two other crosses, and that spear with which our Saviour was struck, and those nails which they drove into His hands and into His feet, and those robes of mockery in which He had been clad; and they hid them: lest, as they said, any one of the kings or of the chief persons should come and inquire concerning the putting to death of Christ.

And the guards went in and said to the priests: Mary cometh in the evening and in the morning, and prayeth there. And there was a commotion in Jerusalem on account of Marath Mary. And the priests went to the judge, and said to him: My lord, send and command Mary that she go not to pray at the sepulchre and at Golgotha. And while they were deliberating, lo! letters came from Abgar, the king of the city of Edessa, to Sabina the procurator[4] who had been appointed by Tiberius the emperor, and as far as the river Euphrates the procurator Sabina had authority. And,

---

[1] From Cod. Add. 16,484, fol. 19. It consists of an apocryphal work on the Virgin, of the fifth or sixth century.

[2] [*i.e.* "My Lady" or "Madam" (= mea domina): it is the feminine form of "Mar."]

[3] [Beginning with the new moon of October. The *former Tishrin* was the month immediately preceding.]

[4] [The Greek ἐπίτροπος is used.]

because Addæus the apostle, one of the seventy-two apostles, had gone down and built a church at Edessa, and had cured the disease with which Abgar the king was afflicted—for Abgar the king loved Jesus Christ, and was constantly inquiring about Him; and, when Christ was put to death and Abgar the king heard that the Jews had slain Him on the cross, he was much displeased; and Abgar arose and rode and came as far as the river Euphrates, because he wished to go up against Jerusalem and lay it waste; and, when Abgar came and was arrived at the river Euphrates, he deliberated in his mind: If I pass over, there will be enmity between me and Tiberius the emperor. And Abgar wrote letters and sent them to Sabina the procurator, and Sabina sent them to Tiberius the emperor. In this manner did Abgar write to Tiberius the emperor:

From Abgar, the king of the city of Edessa. Much peace to thy Majesty, our lord Tiberius! In order that thy Majesty may not be offended with me, I have not passed over the river Euphrates: for I have been wishing to go up against Jerusalem and lay her waste, forasmuch as she has slain Christ, a skilful healer. But do thou, as a great sovereign who hast authority over all the earth and over us, send and do me judgment on the people of Jerusalem. For be it known to thy Majesty that I desire that thou wilt do me judgment on the crucifiers.

And Sabina received the letters, and sent them to Tiberius the emperor. And, when he had read them, Tiberius the emperor was greatly incensed, and he desired to destroy and slay all the Jews. And the people of Jerusalem heard it and were alarmed. And the priests went to the governor, and said to him: My lord, send and command Mary that she go not to pray at the sepulchre and Golgotha. The judge said to the priests: Go ye yourselves, and give her what command and what caution ye please.

VII.[1]

From the Homily composed by the holy Mar Jacob, the teacher, on the Fall of Idols.

To Edessa he made his journey, and found in it a great work [going on]:
For the king was become a labourer for the church, and was building it.
The apostle Addæus stood in it like a builder,
And King Abgar laid aside his diadem and builded with him.
When apostle and king concurred the one with the other,
What idol must not fall before them?
Satan fled to the land of Babylon from the disciples,
And the tale of the crucifixion had got before him to the country of the Chaldeans.
He said, when they were making sport of the signs of the Zodiac, that he was nothing.

VIII.[2]

From the Homily about the town of Antioch.

To Simon was allotted Rome, and to John Ephesus; to Thomas India, and to Addæus the country of the Assyrians.[3] And, when they were sent each one of them to the district which had been allotted to him, they devoted themselves[4] to bring the [several] countries to discipleship.

[1] From Cod. Add. 14,624, apparently written in the ninth century.

[2] From Cod. Add. 14,590, of the eighth or ninth century.

[3] [This is probably the correct reading: the printed text means "among the Assyrians."]

[4] [Lit. "set their faces."]

APPENDIX.

MARTYRDOM[1] OF THE HOLY CONFESSORS SHAMUNA, GURIA, AND HABIB, FROM SIMEON METAPHRASTES.[2]

In the six hundredth year from the empire of Alexander the Macedonian, when Diocletian had been nine years sovereign of the Romans, and Maximian was consul for the sixth time, and Augar son of Zoaras was prætor, and Cognatus was bishop of the Edessenes, a great persecution was raised against the churches in all the countries which were under the sway of the Romans. The name of Christian was looked upon as execrable, and was assailed and harassed with abuse; while the priests and the monks, on account of their staunch and unconquerable stedfastness, were subjected to shocking punishments, and the pious were at their wits' end with sadness and fear. For, desiring as they did to proclaim the truth because of their yearning affection for Christ, they yet shrunk back from doing so for fear of punishment. For those who took up arms against true religion were bent on making the Christians renounce Christianity and embrace the cause of Saturn and Rhea, whilst the faithful on their part laboured to prove that the objects of heathen worship had no real existence.

---

[1] This piece, [which Cureton gives in Latin], is taken from the well-known work of Surius, *De probatis Sanctorum vitis*. It does not appear who made this Latin translation.

[2] [A celebrated Byzantine writer, who lived in the ninth and tenth centuries. He derives his name from having written paraphrases, or metaphrases, of the lives of the saints. Fabricius gives a list of 539 lives commonly attributed to him.—Dr. W. PLATE, in Smith's *Dict. Biog. and Myth.*]

At this period it was that an accusation was preferred before the judge against Guria and Shamuna. The former was a native of Sarcigitua, and the latter of the village of Ganas; they were, however, both brought up at Edessa—which they call Mesopotamia, because it is situated between the Euphrates and the Tigris: a city previously to this but little known to fame, but which after the struggles of its martyrs obtained universal notoriety. These holy men would not by any means spend their lives in the city, but removing to a distance from it, as those who wished to be at a distance from its turmoils, they made it their aim to be manifest to God only. Guria's purity and lovingness were to him a precious and honourable possession, and from his cultivation of the former the surname of *the pure* was given him: so that from his name you would not have known who he was, but only when you called him by his surname. Shamuna devoted his body and his youthful and active mind to the service of God, and rivalled Guria in excellence of character. Against these men an indictment was laid before the judge, to the effect that they not only pervaded all the country round about Edessa with their teaching and encouraged the people to hold fast their faith, but also led them to look with contempt on their persecutors, and, in order to induce them to set wholly at nought their impiety, taught them agreeably to that which is written: "Trust not in princes—in the sons of men, in whom is no safety."[1] By these representations the judge was wrought up to a high pitch of madness, and gave orders that all those who held the Christian religion in honour and followed the teaching of Shamuna and Guria, together with those who persuaded them to this, should be apprehended, and shut up in safe keeping. The order was carried into effect; and, seizing the opportunity, he had some of them flogged, and others tortured in various ways, and induced them to obey the emperor's command, and then, as if he were behaving kindly and mercifully, he allowed others to go to their homes; but [our two] saints, as being the ringleaders and those who had communicated their piety to

[1] [Ps. cxlvi. 3.]

others, he ordered to be still further maltreated in prison. They, however, rejoiced in the fellowship of martyrdom. For they heard of many in other provinces who had had to pass through the same conflict as themselves: among them Epiphanius and Petrus and the most holy Pamphilus, with many others, at Cæsarea in Palestine; Timotheus at Gaza; at Alexandria the Great [another] Timotheus; Agapetus at Thessalonica; Hesychius at Nicomedia; Philippus at Adrianopolis; at Melitina Petrus; Hermes and his companions in the confines of Martyropolis: all of whom were also encircled with the crown of martyrdom by Dux Heraclianus, along with other confessors too numerous for us to become acquainted with. But we must return to the matters of which we were before speaking.

Antonius, then, the governor of Edessa, having permitted others to return to their homes, had a lofty judgment-seat erected, and ordered the martyrs to be brought before him. The attendants having done as they were bidden, the governor said to the saints: Our most divine emperor commands you to renounce Christianity, of which you are followers, and to pay divine honour to Jupiter by offering incense on the altar. To this Shamuna replied: Far be it from us to abandon the true faith, whereby we hope to obtain immortality, and worship the work of men's hands and a [lifeless] image! The governor said: The emperor's orders must by all means be obeyed. Guria answered: Our pure and divine faith will we never disown, by following the will of men, who are subject to dissolution. For we have a Father in heaven whose will we follow, and He says: "He that shall confess Me before men, him will I also confess before My Father who is in heaven; but he that shall deny Me before men, him will I also deny before My Father and His angels."[1] The judge said: You refuse, then, to obey the will of the emperor? But can you for a moment think, that the purposes of ordinary men and such as have no more power than yourselves are to be really carried into execution, while the commands of those who possess supreme power

---

[1] [Matt. x. 33.]

fall to the ground? They, said the saints, who do the will of the King of kings spurn and reject the will of the flesh. Then, on the governor's threatening them with death unless they obeyed, Shamuna said: We shall not die, O tyrant, if we follow the will of the Creator: nay rather, on the contrary, we shall live; but, if we follow the commands of your emperor, know thou that, even though thou shouldest [not] put us to death, we shall perish miserably all the same.

On hearing this, the governor gave orders to Anovitus the jailor to put them in very safe keeping. For the mind which is naturally inclined to evil cannot bear the truth, any more than diseased eyes the bright beams of the sun. And, when he had done as he was commanded, and the martyrs were in prison, where many other saints also had been previously shut by the soldiers, the Emperor Diocletian sent for Musonius the governor of Antioch and ordered him to go to Edessa and see the Christians who were confined there, whether they were of the common or of the sacred class, and question them about their religion, and deal with them as he should see fit. So he came to Edessa; and he had Shamuna and Guria first of all placed before the tribunal of judgment, and said to them: This, and no less, is the command of the lord of the world, that you make a libation of wine and place incense on the altar of Jupiter. If you refuse to do so, I will destroy you with manifold punishments: for I will tear your bodies to pieces with whips, till I get to your very entrails; and I will not cease pouring boiling lead into your armpits until it reaches even to your bowels; after that, I will hang you up, now by your hands, now by your feet, and I will loosen the fastenings of your joints; and I will invent new and unheard of punishments which you will be utterly unable to endure.

Shamuna answered: We dread "the worm," the threat of which is denounced against those who deny the Lord, and "the fire which is not quenched," more than those tortures which thou hast set before us. For [God] Himself, to whom we offer rational worship, will, first of all, strengthen us to bear these manifold tortures, and will deliver us out of thy hands; and, after that, will also give us to rest in a place of safety, where is the abode of all those who rejoice. Besides, it is against nothing whatever but the body that thou takest up arms: for what possible harm couldst thou do to the soul? since, as long as it resides in the body, it proves superior to torture; and, when it takes its departure, the body has no feeling whatever left. For, "the more our outward man is destroyed, the more is our inward man renewed day by day;"[1] for by means of patience we go through with this contest which is set before us. The governor, however, again, with a kind of protestation, in order that, in case they did not obey, he might with the more justice punish them, said: Give up your error, I beg you, and yield to the command of the emperor: ye will not be able to endure the tortures. The holy Guria answered: We are neither the slaves of error, as thou sayest, nor will we ever obey the command of the emperor: God forbid that we should be so weak-minded and so senseless! For we are His disciples who laid down His life for us, so manifesting the riches of His goodness and His love towards us. We will, therefore, resist sin even to death, nor, come what may, will we be foiled by the stratagems of the adversary, by which the first man was ensnared and plucked death from the tree through his disobedience;[2] and Cain was persuaded, and, after staining his hands with his brother's blood, found the rewards of sin to be wailing and fear. But we, listening to the words of Christ, will "not be afraid of those that kill the body but are not able to kill the soul:" Him rather will we fear "who is able to destroy our soul and body."[3] The tyrant said: It is not to give you an opportunity of disproving my allegations by snatches of your own writings that I refrain from anger and show myself forbearing; but that you may per-

---

[1] [2 Cor. iv. 16.]

[2] [Or "through his disobedience in the matter of the tree," if *per ligni inobedientiam* are the real words of the translator, who is not, generally speaking, to be complimented for elegance or even correctness, but seems to have made a servile copy of the mere words of the Greek.]

[3] [Matt. x. 28.]

form the command of the emperor and return in peace to your homes.

These words did not at all shake the resolution of the martyrs; but, approaching nearer: What, said they, does it matter to us, if thou *art* angry, and nursest thine anger, and rainest tortures upon us like snow-flakes? For then wouldst thou be favouring us all the more, by rendering the proof of our fortitude more conspicuous, and winning for us a greater recompense. For this is the crowning point of our hope, that we shall leave behind our present dwelling, which is but for a time, and depart to one that will last for ever. For we have " a tabernacle not made with hands "[1] in heaven, which the Scripture is accustomed also to call " Abraham's bosom," because of the familiar intercourse with God with which he was blessed. The governor, seeing that their firmness underwent no change, forthwith left off speaking and proceeded with the threatened punishments, giving orders to the jailor Anuinus that they should be severally hung up by one hand, and that, when their hands were dislocated by having to bear the entire weight of the body, he should further suspend a heavy stone to their feet, that the sense of pain might be the sharper. This was done, and from the third hour to the eighth they bore this severe torture with fortitude, uttering not a word, nor a groan, nor giving any other indication of a weak or abject mind. You would have said that they were suffering in a body which was not theirs, or that others were suffering and they themselves were nothing more than spectators of what was going on.

In the meantime, whilst they were hanging by their hands, the governor was engaged in trying other cases. Having done with these, he ordered the jailor to inquire of the saints whether or not they would obey the emperor and be released from their torture; and on his putting the question to them, when it was found that they either could not or would not return an answer, he ordered that they should be confined in the inner part of the prison, in a dark dungeon, dark both in name and in reality, and that their feet should be made

[1 2 Cor. v. 1.]

fast in the stocks. At dawn of day, their feet were loosened from the confinement of the stocks; but their prison was close shut up, so that not a single ray even of sunlight could make its way in; and the jailors were ordered not to give them a bit of bread or a single drop of water for three whole days. So that, in addition to all the rest, the martyrs were condemned to a dark prison and a long privation of food. When the third day arrived, about the beginning of the month of August, the prison was opened to admit light, but they were detained in it still up to the 10th of November. Then the judge had them brought up before his tribunal: Has not all this time, said he, sufficed to induce you to change your minds and come to some [more] wholesome decision? They answered: We have already several times told thee our mind : do, therefore, what thou hast been commanded. The governor forthwith ordered that Shamuna should be made to kneel down on one side[1] and that an iron chain should be fastened on his knee. This having been done, he hung him up head downwards by the foot with which he had made him kneel; the other he pulled downwards with a heavy piece of iron, which cannot be described in words: thus endeavouring to rend the champion in twain. By this means the socket of the hip-bone was wrenched out of its place and Shamuna became lame. Guria, however, because he was weak and somewhat pale, he left unpunished : not that he regarded him with friendly eyes—not that he had any compassion on his weakness; but rather by way of sparing for another opportunity one whom he was anxious to punish : lest perchance, as he said, through inadvertence on my part he should be worn out before he has undergone the torments in reserve for him.

By this time two hours of the day had passed since Shamuna had been hung up; and the fifth hour had now arrived, and he was still suspended on high—when the soldiers who stood around, taking pity upon him, urged him to obey the emperor's command. But the compassion of sinners had no effect upon the saint. For, although he suffered bitterly

[1] [Lit. "with one foot."]

from the torture, he vouchsafed them no answer whatever, leaving them to lament at their leisure, and to deem themselves rather, and not him, deserving of pity. But, lifting his eyes to heaven, he prayed to God from the depth of his heart, reminding Him of the wonders done in old time: Lord God, he said, without whom not even a poor little sparrow falls into the snare; who didst cheer the heart of David amid his afflictions; who gavest power to Daniel even against the lions; who madest the children of Abraham victorious over the tyrant and the flame: do Thou now also, O Lord, look on the war which is being waged against us, acquainted as Thou art with the weakness of our nature. For the enemy is trying to turn away the workmanship of Thy right hand from the glory which is with Thee. But regard Thou us with looks of compassion, and maintain within us, against all attempts to extinguish it, the lamp of Thy commandments; and by Thy light guide our paths, and vouchsafe us the enjoyment of that happiness which is in Thee: for Thou art blessed for ever, world without end. Thus did he utter the praise of the Umpire of the strife; and a scribe who was present took down in writing what was said

At length the governor ordered the jailor to release him from his punishment. He did so, and carried him away all faint and exhausted with the pain he suffered, and they bore him back to his former prison and laid him down by the side of the holy Guria. On the 15th of November, however, in the night, about the time of cock-crowing, the judge got up. He was preceded by torches and attendants; and, on arriving at the Basilica, as it is called, where the court was held, he took his seat with great ceremony on the tribunal, and sent to fetch the champions Guria and Shamuna. The latter came in walking between two [of the jailors] and supported by the hands of both: for he was worn out with hunger and weighed down with age: nothing but his good hope sustained him. Guria, too, had also to be carried in: for he could not walk at all, because his foot had been severely galled by the chain on it. Addressing them both, the advocate of impiety said: In pursuance of the permission which was granted, you have, [I presume], consulted together about what it is expedient for you to do. Tell me, then, whether any fresh resolution has been come to by you, and whether you have in any respect changed your mind in regard to your former purpose; and obey the command of the most divine [emperor]. For thus will you be restored to the enjoyment of your property and possessions, yea of this most cheering light also. To this the martyrs reply: No one who is wise would make any great account of continuing for a little while in the enjoyment of things which are but transient. Sufficient for us is the time already past for the use and the sight of them; nor do we feel the want of any of them. That death, on the contrary, with which thou art threatening us will convey us to imperishable habitations and give us a participation in the happiness which is yonder.

The governor replied: What you have said has filled my ears with great sadness. However, I will explain to you what is determined on: if you place incense on the altar and sacrifice to the image of Jupiter, all will be well, and each of you will go away to his home; but, if you still persist in disobeying the command of the emperor, you will most certainly lose your heads: for this is what the great emperor wills and determines. To this the most noble-minded Shamuna replied: If thou shalt confer upon us so great a favour as to grant us deliverance from the miseries of this life and dismissal to the happiness of the life yonder, so far as in us lies thou shalt be rewarded by Him who lays out our possessions on what is for our good. The governor replied to this somewhat kindly, as it seemed, saying: I have patiently endured hitherto, putting up with those long speeches of yours, in order that by delay you may change your purpose and betake yourselves to what is for your good, and not have to undergo the punishment of death. Those who submit, said he, to death which is only for a time, for the sake of Christ, will manifestly be delivered from eternal death. For those who die to the world live in Christ. For Peter also, who shines so brightly among the band of apostles, was condemned to the cross and to death; and James, the son of thunder, was slain by Herod Agrippa with the sword. Moreover, Stephen also was stoned, who was the first to run the course of martyrdom. What, too, wilt thou say of John [the Baptist]? Thou wilt surely acknowledge his distinguished fortitude and boldness of speech, when he preferred death rather than keep silence about conjugal infidelity, and the adulteress received his head as a reward for her dancing?

Again the governor said: It is not that you may reckon up your saints, as you call them, that I bear so patiently with you, but that, by changing your resolution and yielding to the emperor's commands, you may be rescued from a very bitter death. For, if you behave with such excessive daring and arrogance, what can you expect but that severer punishments are in store for you, under the pressure of which you will be ready even against your will to do what I demand of you: by which time, however, it will be altogether too late to take refuge in compassion? For the cry which is wrung from you by force has no power to challenge pity; whilst, on the other hand, that which is made of your own accord is deserving of compassion. The confessors and martyrs of Christ said: There needs not many words. For lo! we are ready to undergo all the punishments thou mayest lay upon us. What, therefore, has been commanded thee, delay not to perform. For we are the worshippers of Christ the true God, and (again we say it) of Him of whose kingdom there shall be no end; who also is alone able to glorify those in return who glorify His name. In the meantime, whilst these things were being said by the saints, the governor pronounced sentence against them that they should suffer death by the sword. But they, filled with a joy beyond the power of words to express, exclaimed: To Thee of right belongeth glory and praise, who art God of all, because it hath pleased Thee that we should carry on to its close the conflict we have entered upon, and that we should also receive at Thy hands the brightness that shall never fade away.

When, therefore, the governor saw their unyielding firmness, and how they had heard the final sentence with exultation of soul, he said to the saints: May God search into what is being done, [and be witness] that so far as I was concerned it was no wish of mine that you should lose your lives; but the inflexible command of the emperor to me compels me to this. He then ordered a halberdier to take charge of the martyrs, and, putting them in a carriage, to convey them to a distance from the city with some soldiers, and there to end them with the sword. So he, taking the saints out at night by the Roman gate, when the citizens were buried in profound slumber, conveyed them to Mount Bethelabicla on the north of the city. On their arrival at that place, having alighted from the carriage with joy of heart and great firmness of mind, they requested the halberdier and those who were under his orders to give them time to pray; and it was granted. For, just as if their tortures and their blood were not enough to plead for them, they still by reason of their humility deemed it necessary to pray. So they raised their eyes to heaven and prayed earnestly, concluding with the words: God and Father of our Lord Jesus Christ, receive in peace our spirits to Thyself. Then Shamuna, turning to the halberdier, said: Perform that which thou hast been commanded. So he kneeled down along with Guria, and they were beheaded, on the 15th of November. This is the account of what happened to the martyrs.

But forasmuch as the number sought for a third in order that in them the Trinity might be glorified, it found, oh admirable providence! Habib—at a subsequent time indeed: but he also, along with those who had preceded him, had determined to enter on the journey, and on the very day[1] of their martyrdom reached his consummation. Habib, then, great among martyrs, was a native of the same place as they, namely of the village of Thelsæa;[2] and he had the honour of being invested with the sacred office of the diaconate. But, when Licinius swayed the sceptre of the Roman empire and Lysanias had been appointed governor of Edessa, a persecution was again raised against the Christians, and the

---

[1] [*i.e.* the anniversary.]
[2] [In the Syriac account "Telzcha:" see p. 91.]

general danger threatened Habib. For he would go about the city, teaching the divine Scriptures to all he met with, and courageously seeking to strengthen them in [the practice of] piety. When this came to the ears of Lysanias, he gave information of it to the Emperor Licinius. For he was anxious to be himself entrusted with the business of bringing the Christians to trial, and especially Habib: for he had never been entrusted with it before. The emperor, then, sent him a letter and commanded him to put Habib to death. So, when Lysanias had received the letter, search was made everywhere for Habib, who on account of his office in the church lived in some part of the city, his mother and some of his relations residing with him. When he got intelligence of the matter, fearing lest he should incur punishment for quitting the ranks of martyrdom, he went of his own accord and presented himself to a man who was among the chief of the body-guard, named Theotecnus, and presently he said: I am Habib for whom ye are seeking. But he, looking kindly at him, said: No one, my good man, is as yet aware of thy coming to me: so go away, and look to thy safety; and be not concerned about thy mother, nor about thy relations: for they cannot possibly get into any trouble. Thus far Theotecnus.

But Habib, because the occasion was one that called for martyrdom, refused to yield to a weak and cowardly spirit and secure his safety in any underhand way. He replied, therefore: It is not for the sake of my dear mother, nor for the sake of my kinsfolk, that I denounce myself; but I have come for the sake of the confession of Christ. For lo! whether thou consent or no, I will make my appearance before the governor, and I will proclaim my [Lord] Christ before princes and kings. Theotecnus, accordingly, apprehensive that he might go of his own accord to the governor, and that in this way he might himself be in jeopardy for not having denounced him, took Habib and conducted him to the governor: Here, said he, is Habib, for whom search has been made. When Lysanias learned that Habib had come of his own accord to the contest, he concluded that this was a mark of contempt and overweening boldness, as if he set light by the solemn dignity of the judicial seat; and he had him at once put on his trial. He inquired of him his condition of life, his name, and his country. On his answering that he was a native of the village of Thelsæa, and intimating that he was a minister of Christ, the governor immediately charged the martyr with not obeying the emperor's commands. He insisted that a plain proof of this was his refusal to offer incense to Jupiter. To this Habib kept replying that he was a Christian, and could not forsake the true God, or sacrifice to the lifeless works of [men's] hands which had no sensation. The governor hereupon ordered, that his arms should be bound with ropes, and that he should be raised up high on a beam and torn with iron claws.[1] The hanging up was far more difficult to bear than the tearing: for he was in danger of being pulled asunder, through the forcible strain with which his arms were stretched out.

In the meantime, as he was hanging up in the air, the governor had recourse to smooth words, and assumed the guise of patience. He, however, continued to threaten him with severer punishments unless he should change his resolution. But he said: No man shall induce me to forsake the faith, nor persuade me to worship demons, even though he should inflict tortures more and greater. On the governor's asking him what advantage he expected to gain from tortures which destroyed his whole[2] body, Habib, Christ's martyr, replied: The objects of our regard do not last merely for the present, nor do we pursue the things that are seen; and, if thou too art minded to turn thy look towards our hope and promised recompense, possibly thou wilt even say with Paul: "The sufferings of this time are not worthy to be compared with the glory which is to be revealed in us."[3] The governor pronounced his words to be the language of imbecility; and, when he saw that, notwithstanding all the efforts he made, by turns using smooth words and assuming

---

[1] [Compare the "combs" of the Syriac, *supra*.]
[2] [Reading "totum" for "solum."]
[3] [Rom. viii. 18.]

the part of patience, and then again threatening him and menacing him with a shocking[1] death, he could not in either way prevail with him, he said, as he pronounced sentence upon him: I will not inflict on thee a sudden and speedy death; I will bring on thy dissolution gradually by means of a slow fire, and in this way make thee lay aside thy fierce and intractable spirit. Thereupon, some wood was collected together at a place outside the city on the northward, and he was led to the pile, followed by his mother, and also by those who were otherwise by blood related to him. He then prayed, and pronounced a blessing on all, and gave them the kiss in the Lord; and after that the wood was kindled by them, and he was cast into the fire; and, when he had opened his mouth to receive the flame, he yielded up his spirit to Him who had given it. Then, when the fire had subsided, his relatives wrapped him in a costly piece of linen and anointed him with unguents; and, having suitably sung psalms and hymns, they laid him by the side of Shamuna and Guria, to the glory of the Father, and of the Son, and of the Holy Spirit, who constitute a Divine Trinity, which cannot be divided: to whom is due honour and worship now and always, and for evermore, Amen. Such was the close of the life of the martyr Habib in the time of Licinius, and thus did he obtain the privilege of being laid with the saints, and thus did he bring to the pious rest from their persecutions. For shortly afterwards the power of Licinius waned, and the rule of Constantine prospered, and the sovereignty of the Romans became his; and he was the first of the emperors who openly professed piety, and allowed the Christians to live as Christians.

[1] [Lit. " bitter."]

MOSES OF CHORENE.[1]
HISTORY OF ARMENIA.
BOOK II.—CHAPTER XXVI.

Reign of Abgar—Armenia becomes completely tributary to the Romans—War with Herod's troops—His brother's son, Joseph, is killed.

Abgar, son of Archam, ascends the throne in the twentieth year of Archavir, king of the Persians. This Abgar was called Avak-aïr (great man), on account of his great gentleness and wisdom, and also on account of his size. Not being able to pronounce well, the Greeks and the Syrians called him Abgar. In the second year of his reign, all the districts of Armenia become tributary to the Romans. A command is given by the Emperor Augustus, as we are told in the Gospel of St. Luke, to number all the people in every part. Roman commissioners, sent for that purpose into Armenia, carried thither the statue of the Emperor Augustus, and set it up in all the temples. At this very time, our Saviour Jesus Christ, the Son of God, came into the world.

At the same period there was trouble between Abgar and Herod: for Herod wished that his statue should be erected near to that of Cæsar in the temples of Armenia. Abgar withstood this claim. Moreover, Herod was but seeking a pretext to attack Abgar: he sent an army of Thracians and Germans to make an incursion into the country of the Persians, with orders to pass through the territories of Abgar. But Abgar, far from submitting to this, resisted, saying that the emperor's command was to march the troops into Persia through the desert. Herod, indignant, and unable to act by himself, overwhelmed with troubles, as a punishment for his wicked conduct towards Christ, as Josephus relates, sent his nephew to whom he had given his daughter, who had been

---

[1] This extract is taken from the edition, in two volumes, printed at Paris, of which the following is the title: MOÏSE DE KHORÈNE, *auteur du Ve Siècle*: HISTOIRE D'ARMÉNIE, TEXTE ARMÉNIEN ET TRADUCTION FRANCAISE, *avec notes explicatives et précis historiques sur l'Arménie*, par P. E. LE VAILLANT DE FLORIVAL.

married in the first instance to Phéror, his brother. Herod's lieutenant, at the head of a considerable army, hastened to reach Mesopotamia, met Abgar at the camp in the province of Pouknan, fell in the combat, and his troops were put to flight. Soon afterwards, Herod died: Archelaus, his son, was appointed by Augustus ethnarch of Judæa.

CHAPTER XXVII.

Founding of the town of Edessa—Brief account of the race of our Illuminator.

A little while afterwards, Augustus dies, and Tiberius becomes emperor of the Romans in his stead. Germanicus, having become Cæsar, dragging in his train the princes of the kingdom of Archavir and of Abgar, celebrates a triumph in respect of the war waged with them, in which these princes had killed Herod's nephew. Abgar, indignant, forms plans of revolt and prepares himself for combat. He builds a town on the ground occupied by the Armenian army of observation, where previously the Euphrates had been defended against the attempts of Cassius: this new town is called Edessa. Abgar removed to it his court, which was at Medzpine, all his gods, Naboc, Bel, Patnicagh, and Tarata, the books of the schools attached to the temples, and even the royal archives.

After this, Archavir being dead, Ardachès, his son, reigns over the Persians. Though it is not in the order of the history with respect to time, nor even the order according to which we have begun these annals, yet, as we are treating of the descendants of the king Archavir, even of the blood of Ardachès his son, we will, to do honour to these princes, place them, by anticipating the time, near to Ardachès, in order that the reader may know that they are of the same race, of the race of the brave Archag; then we will indicate the time of the arrival of their fathers in Armenia, the Garenians and the Sourenians, from whom St. Gregory and the Gamsarians are descended, when, following the order of events, we come to the reign of the king under whom they appeared.

Abgar did not succeed in his plans of revolt; for, troubles having arisen amongst his relatives in the Persian kingdom, he set out at the head of an army to allay and bring to an end the dissension.

CHAPTER XXVIII.

Abgar comes into the East, maintains Ardachès upon the throne of Persia—Reconciles his brothers from whom our Illuminator and his relations are descended.

Abgar, having gone to the East, finds on the throne of Persia Ardachès, son of Archavir, and the brothers of Ardachès contending against him: for this prince thought to reign over them in his posterity, and they would not consent to it. Ardachès therefore hems them in on all sides, hangs the sword of death over their heads; distractions and dissension were between their troops and their other relations and allies: for king Archavir had three sons and one daughter; the first of these sons was King Ardachès himself, the second Garène, the third Sourène; their sister, named Gochm, was wife of the general of all the Ariks, a general chosen by their father Archavir.

Abgar prevails on the sons of Archavir to make peace; he arranges between them the conditions and stipulations: Ardachès is to reign with his posterity as he proposed, and his brothers are to be called Bahlav, from the name of their town and their vast and fertile country, so that their satrapies shall be the first, higher in rank than all the satrapies of Persia, as being truly a race of kings. Treaties and oaths stipulated that in case of the extinction of male children of Ardachès, his brothers should come to the throne; after the reigning race of Ardachès, his brothers are divided into three races named thus: the race of Garène Bahlav, the race of Sourène Bahlav, and the race of their sister, the race of Asbahabied Bahlav, a race thus called from the name of the domain of her husband.

St. Gregory is said to have sprung from the race Sourène Bahlav, and the Gamsarians from the race Garène Bahlav.

We will relate in the sequel the circumstances of the coming of these personages, only mentioning their names here in connection with Ardachès, in order that you may know that these great races are indeed the blood of Vagharchag, that is to say, the posterity of the great Archag, brother of Vagharchag.

Everything being thus arranged, Abgar takes with him the letter of the treaties, and returns to his dominions, not in perfect health, but a prey to severe suffering.

CHAPTER XXIX.

Abgar returns from the East—He gives help to Aretas in a war against Herod the tetrarch.

When Abgar had returned from the East, he learnt that the Romans suspected him of having gone there to raise troops. He therefore made the Roman commissioners acquainted with the reasons of his journey to Persia, as well as the treaty concluded between Ardachès and his brothers; but no credence was given to his statement: for he was accused by his enemies Pilate, Herod the tetrarch, Lysanias and Philip. Abgar having returned to his city Edessa leagued himself with Aretas, king of Petra, and gave him some auxiliary troops under the command of Khosran Ardzrouni, to make war upon Herod. Herod had in the first instance married the daughter of Aretas, then had repudiated her, and thereupon taken Herodias, even in her husband's lifetime, a circumstance in connection with which he had had John the Baptist put to death. Consequently there was war between Herod and Aretas on account of the wrong done to the daughter of Aretas. Being sharply attacked, Herod's troops were defeated, thanks to the help of the brave Armenians; as if, by divine providence, vengeance was taken for the death of John the Baptist.

CHAPTER XXX.

Abgar sends princes to Marinus—These deputies see our Saviour Christ—Beginning of the conversion of Abgar.

At this period Marinus, son of Storoge, was raised by the emperor to the government of Phœnicia, Palestine, Syria, and Mesopotamia. Abgar sent to him two of his principal officers, Mar-Ihap prince of Aghtznik, and Chamchacram chief of the house of the Abahouni, as well as Anan his confidant. The envoys proceed to the town of Petkoupine to make known to Marinus the reasons of Abgar's journey to the East, showing him the treaty concluded between Ardachès and his brothers, and at the same time to call upon Marinus for his support. The deputies found the Roman governor at Eleutheropolis; he received them with friendship and distinction, and gave this answer to Abgar: "Fear nothing from the emperor on that account, provided you take good care to pay the tribute regularly."

On their return, the Armenian deputies went to Jerusalem to see our Saviour the Christ, being attracted by the report of His miracles. Having themselves become eye-witnesses of these wonders, they related them to Abgar. This prince, seized with admiration, believed truly that Jesus was indeed the Son of God, and said: "These wonders are not those of a man, but of a God. No, there is no one amongst men who can raise the dead: God alone has this power." Abgar felt in his whole body certain acute pains which he had got in Persia, more than seven years before; from men he had received no remedy for his sufferings; Abgar sent a letter of entreaty to Jesus: he prayed Him to come and cure him of his pains. Here is this letter:—

CHAPTER XXXI.

Abgar's letter to the Saviour Jesus Christ.

"Abgar, son of Archam, prince of the land, to Jesus, Saviour and Benefactor of men, who has appeared in the country of Jerusalem, greeting:

"I have heard of Thee, and of the cures wrought by Thy hands, without remedies, without herbs : for, as it is said, Thou makest the blind to see, the lame to walk, the lepers to be healed ; Thou drivest out unclean spirits, Thou curest unhappy beings afflicted with prolonged and inveterate diseases ; Thou dost even raise the dead. As I have heard of all these wonders wrought by Thee, I have concluded from them either that Thou art God, come down from heaven to do such great things, or that Thou art the Son of God, working as Thou dost these miracles. Therefore have I written to Thee, praying Thee to condescend to come to me and cure me of the complaints with which I am afflicted. I have heard also that the Jews murmur against Thee and wish to deliver Thee up to torments : I have a city small but pleasant, it would be sufficient for us both."

The messengers, the bearers of this letter, met Jesus at Jerusalem, a fact confirmed by these words of the Gospel : "Some from amongst the heathen came to find Jesus, but those who heard them, not daring to tell Jesus what they had heard, told it to Philip and Andrew, who repeated it all to their Master."

The Saviour did not then accept the invitation given to Him, but He thought fit to honour Abgar with an answer in these words :—

CHAPTER XXXII.

Answer to Abgar's letter, which the Apostle Thomas wrote to this prince by command of the Saviour.

"Blessed is he who believes in me without having seen me ! For it is written of me : 'Those who see me will not believe in me, and those who do not see me will believe and live.' As to what thou hast written asking me to come to thee, I must accomplish here all that for which I have been sent ; and, when I shall have accomplished it all, I shall ascend to Him who sent me ; and when I shall go away I will send one of my disciples, who will cure thy diseases, and give life to thee and to all those who are with thee." Anan, Abgar's courier, brought him this letter, as well as the portrait of the

Saviour, a picture which is still to be found at this day in the city of Edessa.

CHAPTER XXXIII.

Preaching of the Apostle Thaddeus at Edessa—Copy of five letters.

After the ascension of our Saviour, the Apostle Thomas, one of the twelve, sent one of the seventy-six disciples, Thaddeus, to the city of Edessa to heal Abgar and to preach the gospel, according to the word of the Lord. Thaddeus came to the house of Tobias, a Jewish prince, who is said to have been of the race of the Pacradouni. Tobias, having left Archam, did not abjure Judaism with the rest of his relatives, but followed its laws up to the moment when he believed in Christ. Soon the name of Thaddeus spreads through the whole town. Abgar, on learning of his arrival, said: "This is indeed he concerning whom Jesus wrote to me;" and immediately Abgar sent for the apostle. When Thaddeus entered, a marvellous appearance presented itself to the eyes of Abgar in the countenance of the apostle; the king having risen from his throne, fell on his face to the earth, and prostrated himself before Thaddeus. This spectacle greatly surprised all the princes who were present, for they were ignorant of the fact of the vision. "Art thou really," said Abgar to Thaddeus, "art thou the disciple of the ever-blessed Jesus? Art thou he whom He promised to send to me, and canst thou heal my maladies?" "Yes," answered Thaddeus; "if thou believest in Jesus Christ, the Son of God, the desires of thy heart shall be granted." "I have believed in Jesus," said Abgar, "I have believed in His Father; therefore I wished to go at the head of my troops to destroy the Jews who have crucified Jesus, had I not been prevented by reason of the power of the Romans."

Thenceforth Thaddeus began to preach the gospel to the king and his town; laying his hands upon Abgar, he cured him; he cured also a man with gout, Abdu, a prince of the town, much honoured in all the king's house. He also healed all the sick and infirm people in the town, and all believed in Jesus Christ. Abgar was baptized, and all the town with him, and the temples of the false gods were closed, and all the statues of idols that were placed on the altars and columns were hidden by being covered with reeds. Abgar did not compel any one to embrace the faith, yet from day to day the number of the believers was multiplied.

The Apostle Thaddeus baptizes a manufacturer of silk head-dresses, called Attæus, consecrates him, appoints him [to minister] at Edessa, and leaves him with the king instead of himself. Thaddeus, after having received letters patent from Abgar, who wished that all should listen to the gospel of Christ, went to find Sanadroug, son of Abgar's sister, whom this prince had appointed over the country and over the army. Abgar was pleased to write to the Emperor Tiberius a letter in these words:—

Abgar's letter to Tiberius.

"Abgar, king of Armenia, to my lord Tiberius, emperor of the Romans, greeting:

"I know that nothing is unknown to your Majesty, but, as your friend, I would make you better acquainted with the facts by writing. The Jews who dwell in the cantons of Palestine have crucified Jesus: Jesus without sin, Jesus after so many acts of kindness, so many wonders and miracles wrought for their good, even to the raising of the dead. Be assured that these are not the effects of the power of a simple mortal, but of God. During the time that they were crucifying Him, the sun was darkened, the earth was moved, shaken; Jesus Himself, three days afterwards, rose from the dead and appeared to many. Now, everywhere, His name alone, invoked by His disciples, produces the greatest miracles: what has happened to myself is the most evident proof of it. Your august Majesty knows henceforth what ought to be done in future with respect to the Jewish nation, which has committed this crime; your Majesty knows whether a command should not be published through the whole universe to worship Christ as the true God. Safety and health."

Answer from Tiberius to Abgar's letter.

"Tiberius, emperor of the Romans, to Abgar, king of the Armenians, greeting:

"Your kind letter has been read to me, and I wish that thanks should be given to you from me. Though we had already heard several persons relate these facts, Pilate has officially informed us of the miracles of Jesus. He has certified to us that after his resurrection from the dead he was acknowledged by many to be God. Therefore I myself also wished to do what you propose; but, as it is the custom of the Romans not to admit a god merely by the command of the sovereign, but only when the admission has been discussed and examined in full senate, I proposed the affair to the senate, and they rejected it with contempt, doubtless because it had not been considered by them first. But we have commanded all those whom Jesus suits, to receive him amongst the gods. We have threatened with death any one who shall speak evil of the Christians. As to the Jewish nation which has dared to crucify Jesus, who, as I hear, far from deserving the cross and death, was worthy of honour, worthy of the adoration of men—when I am free from the war with rebellious Spain, I will examine into the matter, and will treat the Jews as they deserve."

Abgar writes another letter to Tiberius.

"Abgar, king of the Armenians, to my lord Tiberius, emperor of the Romans, greeting:

"I have received the letter written from your august Majesty, and I have applauded the commands which have emanated from your wisdom. If you will not be angry with me, I will say that the conduct of the senate is extremely ridiculous and absurd: for, according to the senators, it is after the examination and by the suffrages of men that divinity may be ascribed. Thus, then, if God does not suit man, He cannot be God, since God is to be judged and justified by man. It will no doubt seem just to my lord and master to send another governor to Jerusalem in the place of Pilate, who ought to be ignominiously driven from the powerful post in which you placed him; for he has done the will of the Jews: he has crucified Christ unjustly, without your order. That you may enjoy health is my desire."

Abgar, having written this letter, placed a copy of it, with copies of the other letters, in his archives. He wrote also to the young Nerseh, king of Assyria, at Babylon:—

Abgar's letter to Nerseh.

"Abgar, king of the Armenians, to my son Nerseh, greeting:

"I have received your letter and acknowledgments. I have released Beroze from his chains, and have pardoned his offences: if this pleases you, give him the government of Nineveh. But as to what you write to me about sending you the physician who works miracles and preaches another God superior to fire and water, that you may see and hear him, I say to you: he was not a physician according to the art of men; he was a disciple of the Son of God, Creator of fire and water: he has been appointed and sent to the countries of Armenia. But one of his principal companions, named Simon, is sent into the countries of Persia. Seek for him, and you will hear him, you as well as your father Ardachès. He will heal all your diseases and will show you the way of life."

Abgar wrote also to Ardachès, king of the Persians, the following letter:—

Abgar's letter to Ardachès.

"Abgar, king of the Armenians, to Ardachès my brother, king of the Persians, greeting:

"I know that you have heard of Jesus Christ, the Son of God, whom the Jews have crucified, Jesus who was raised from the dead, and has sent His disciples through all the world to instruct men. One of His chief disciples, named Simon, is in your Majesty's territories. Seek for him, and you will find him, and he will cure you of all your maladies, and will show you the way of life, and you will believe in his words, you, and your brothers, and all those who willingly obey you. It is very pleasant to me to think that my relations in the flesh will be also my relations, my friends, in the spirit."

Abgar had not yet received answers to these letters when he died, having reigned thirty-eight years.

CHAPTER XXXIV.

Martyrdom of our Apostles.

After the death of Abgar, the kingdom of Armenia was divided between two: Ananoun, Abgar's son, reigned at Edessa, and his sister's son, Sanadroug, in Armenia. What took place in their time has been previously told by others: the apostle's arrival in Armenia, the conversion of Sanadroug and his apostasy for fear of the Armenian satraps, and the martyrdom of the apostle and his companions in the canton of Chavarchan, now called Ardaz, and the stone opening to receive the body of the apostle, and the removal of this body by his disciples, his burial in the plain, and the martyrdom of the king's daughter, Santoukhd, near the road, and the apparition of the remains of the two saints, and their removal to the rocks—all circumstances related by others, as we have said, a long time before us: we have not thought it important to repeat them here. In the same way also what is related of the martyrdom at Edessa of Attæus, a disciple of the apostle, a martyrdom ordered by Abgar's son, has been told by others before us.

The prince who reigned after the death of his father, did not inherit his father's virtues: he opened the temples of the idols, and embraced the religion of the heathen. He sent word to Attæus: "Make me a head-dress of cloth interwoven with gold, like those you formerly used to make for my father." He received this answer from Attæus: "My hands shall not make a head-dress for an unworthy prince, who does not worship Christ the living God."

Immediately the king ordered one of his armed men to

cut off Attæus' feet. The soldier went, and, seeing the holy man seated in the chair of the teacher, cut off his legs with his sword, and immediately the saint gave up the ghost. We mention this cursorily, as a fact related by others a long while ago. There came then into Armenia the Apostle Bartholomew, who suffered martyrdom among us in the town of Arepan. As to Simon, who was sent into Persia, I cannot relate with certainty what he did, nor where he suffered martyrdom. It is said that one Simon, an apostle, was martyred at Veriospore. Is this true, or why did the saint come to this place? I do not know; I have only mentioned this circumstance that you may know I spare no pains to tell you all that is necessary.

CHAPTER XXXV.

Reign of Sanadroug—Murder of Abgar's children—The Princess Helena.

Sanadroug, being on the throne, raises troops with the help of the brave Pacradouni and Ardzrouni, who had exalted him, and goes to wage war upon the children of Abgar, to make himself master of the whole kingdom. Whilst Sanadroug was occupied with these affairs, as if by an effect of divine providence vengeance was taken for the death of Attæus; for a marble column which the son of Abgar was having erected at Edessa, on the summit of his palace, while he was underneath to direct the work, escaped from the hands of the workmen, fell upon him and crushed his feet.

Immediately there came a message from the inhabitants of the town, asking Sanadroug for a treaty by which he should engage not to disturb them in the exercise of the Christian religion, in consideration of which, they would give up the town and the king's treasures. Sanadroug promised, but in the end violated his oath. Sanadroug put all the children of the house of Abgar to the edge of the sword, with the exception of the daughters, whom he withdrew from the town to place them in the canton of Hachdiank. As to the first of Abgar's wives, named Helena, he sent her to his town at Kharan, and left to her the sovereignty of the whole

L

of Mesopotamia, in remembrance of the benefits he had received from Abgar by Helena's means.

Helena, pious like her husband Abgar, did not wish to live in the midst of idolaters; she went away to Jerusalem in the time of Claudius, during the famine which Agabus had predicted; with all her treasures she bought in Egypt an immense quantity of corn, which she distributed amongst the poor, a fact to which Josephus testifies. Helena's tomb, a truly remarkable one, is still to be seen before the gate of Jerusalem.

CHAPTER XXXVI.

Restoration of the town of Medzpine—Name of Sanadroug—His death.

Of all Sanadroug's doings and actions, we judge none worthy of remembrance except the building of the town of Medzpine; for, this town having been shaken by an earthquake, Sanadroug pulled it down, rebuilt it more magnificently, and surrounded it with double walls and ramparts. Sanadroug caused to be erected in the middle of the town his statue holding in his hand a single piece of money, which signifies: "All my treasures have been used in building the town, and no more than this single piece of money is left to me."

But why was this prince called Sanadroug? We will tell you: Because Abgar's sister, Otœa, while travelling in Armenia in the winter, was assailed by a whirlwind of snow in the Gortouk mountains; the tempest separated them all, so that none of them knew where his companion had been driven. The prince's nurse, Sanod, sister of Piourad Pacradouni, wife of Khosran Ardzrouni, having taken the royal infant, for Sanadroug was still in the cradle, laid him upon her bosom, and remained with him under the snow three days and three nights. Legend has taken possession of this circumstance: it relates that an animal, a new species, wonderful, of great whiteness, sent by the gods, guarded the child. But so far as we have been informed, this is the fact: a white dog, which was amongst the men sent in search, found the child and his nurse; the prince was therefore called Sanadroug, a name taken from his nurse's name (and from the Armenian name, *dourk*, a gift), as if to signify the gift of Sanod.

Sanadroug, having ascended the throne in the twelfth year of Ardachès, king of the Persians, and having lived thirty years, died as he was hunting, from an arrow which pierced his bowels, as if in punishment of the torments which he had made his holy daughter suffer. Gheroupna, son of the scribe Apchatar, collected all these facts, happening in the time of Abgar and Sanadroug, and placed them in the archives of Edessa.

[NOTE referred to on p. 39.—The following list of the Syrian names of months, in use in the empire and during the era of the Seleucidæ, several of which have been mentioned in these Documents, is taken from *Caswinii Calendarium Syriacum*, edited in Arabic and Latin by Volck, 1859. The later Hebrew names also are here added for comparison. It must, however, be noticed that "the years employed [in the Syrian Calendar] were, at least after the incarnation, Julian years, composed of Roman months." (See *L'Art de vérifier les dates*: Paris, 1818, tom. i. p. 45.) The correspondence with the Hebrew months, therefore, is not so close as the names would indicate, since these commenced with the new moons, and an intercalary month, Veadar, following their twelfth month Adar, was added.

	SYRIAN.	HEBREW.
October,	Tishri prior.	Tishri (or Ethanim).
November,	Tishri posterior.	Bull (or Marcheshvan).
December,	Canun prior.	Chisleu.
January,	Canun posterior.	Tebeth.
February,	Shubat.	Shebat.
March,	Adar.	Adar.
April,	Nisan.	Nisan.
May,	Ajar.	Zif (or Iyar).
June,	Chaziran.	Sivan.
July,	Tamuz.	Tammuz.
August,	Ab.	Ab.
September,	Elul.	Elul.]

INDEXES.

I.—INDEX OF TEXTS.

1 Samuel.		Matthew.			PAGE
	PAGE		PAGE	xiv. 12,	59
ii. 3,	40	iv. 19,	33	xvi. 4,	43
		iv. 24,	7		
Psalms.		vii. 6,	101	Romans.	
x. 5,	69	x. 28,	140	v. 4,	75
xxxiv. 1,	42	x. 33,	138	vii. 24,	15
cxlvi. 3,	137	x. 39,	101	viii. 18,	100, 148
		xi. 8,	23		
		xxiv. 27,	38	1 Corinthians.	
Proverbs.		xxvii. 52,	11	xv. 19,	15
xix. 25,	16				
		Mark.		2 Corinthians.	
Jeremiah.		v. 15,	23	iv. 16,	140
xvii. 5,	114			v. 1,	141
		Luke.		viii. 12,	89
Daniel.		xxiii. 48,	17		
iv. 13,	85	Acts.		Ephesians.	
iv. 35,	101	i. 12, etc.,	36	i. 18,	18
				ii. 14,	11, 13

II.—INDEX OF PRINCIPAL SUBJECTS.

ABGAR, king of Edessa, meaning of the name, 5; the reign of, 150; trouble between, and Herod, 150; founds Edessa, 150; maintains Ardachès on the throne of Persia, and reconciles his brothers, 152; helps Aretas against Herod the tetrarch, 153; certain envoys of, visit Jerusalem and witness the miracles of Jesus, and relate them to Abgar, who believes, 154; request of, to Jesus, 5, 6; letter of, to Jesus, and the reply, 7, 8, 154, 155, 156; the mission of Thaddæus or Addæus to, 8, 156; the meeting of, and Thaddæus, 9; healed of his disease by Thaddæus, 10, 12; commands money to be given to Thaddæus, who refuses it, 13; Thaddæus preaches before, 13–20; expresses his readiness to favour and aid Thaddæus, 21; the joy of, 22; compels none to profess Christ, 23; message of Narses, or Nersch, king of the Assyrians, to, 26; letter of, to Tiberius, 26, 157; reply of Tiberius to, 26, 27, 158; receives Aristides the messenger of Tiberius, 28; sorrow for the death of Thaddæus, 31, 32; his contumacious son, 34; a second letter of, to Tiberius, 158; letter of, to Nerseh, king of Assyria, 159; letter of, to Ardachès, 159, 160;

division of the kingdom of, after his death, 160; murder of the children of, 161.

Abshelma, made deacon by Addæus, 29.

Addæus. [See *Thaddæus*.]

Aggæus and others cleave to Addæus, 24; appointed guardian and ruler by Addæus, 29; makes priests and guides in the whole country of Mesopotamia, 32; barbarously put to death by a son of Abgar, 34; another statement about, 157.

Ananoun, son of Abgar, 160.

Anovitus, the jailor, 139.

Ansus, appointed by Peter bishop of Rome, 55.

Antonius, governor of Edessa, 138.

Apostate, an, not to be re-admitted to the church, 41.

Apostles, the, the preaching of, 35, etc.; in perplexity as to how they should preach, 37; Simon Cephas' counsels to, 37; the mysterious voice, odour, and tongues which come to, 37; the constitutions or appointments of, 38-43; guides and rulers in the church after the death of, and the writings of, 45; the teaching of, generally believed, 46.

Archavoir, king of Persia, 151.

Ardachês, king of Persia, 151; maintained on the throne by Abgar, 152; letter of Abgar to, 159, 160.

Aretas, aided in a war against Herod the tetrarch, 153.

Aristides, sent by Tiberius to Abgar, 28.

Ascension of Christ, 36.

Avida and Barcalba, ask Addæus questions respecting Christ, 22.

BABAI, sister of Sharbil, put to death along with her brother, 78.

Barsamya, bishop of Edessa, converts Sharbil the pagan high priest, 57-60; accused before the judge Lysinus, 80, 81; the Christians demand to die with him, 81, 82; examined by Lysinus, 82-87; sentenced to be tortured, but the judge receiving letters forbidding the persecution of Christians, he is set free, 87-89.

CANTICLE, the, of Mar Jacob on Edessa, when she sent the request to Christ Jesus to come to her, 129, etc.

Chorepiscopoi, 42, 43.

Christians, the, when about to be banished from Rome, claim the bones of their dead, the removal of which causes earthquakes, etc., 79, 80.

Clergy, orders of, appointed by the apostles, 39; who not to be admitted to, or to be excluded from, 40, 41, 42.

Constantine, 117.

Constitutions of the apostles, 38-43.

DAYS and times of sacred observance, appointed by the apostles, 38, 39.

Dead, the commemoration of the, 41, 42.

Death, contempt of, shown by Christians, 126, 127.

Diocletian, persecution of the Christians under, 136.

Disciples, secret, constrained to confess Christ, 43, 44.

EAST, praying towards the, 38.

Edessa, 5 note, 6 note; succession of the bishops of 89, 90; the founding of, 151; martyrs of, 114.

Epiphany, appointed by the apostles, 39.

FABIANUS, bishop of Rome, 80.

First day of the week, the, appointed by the apostles, 38.

GREGORY, St., his illustrious descent, 152, 153.

Guides and rulers of the church, 32, 39, 45.

Guria and Shamuna, martyrs, indictment brought against, 137; boldness of, before the governor, 138; examination of, by Musonius, governor of Antioch, 139, etc.; tortured, immured in a dungeon, and made fast in the stocks, 141, 142; brought before Musonius again, and examined, 143, 144; their unyielding firmness, 145; beheaded, 146.

HABIB, a deacon, accused to the governor—the family of, arrested, 92; delivers himself up, 93, 94; is examined, scourged, and tor-

INDEX OF PRINCIPAL SUBJECTS. 167

tured, 96-101; sentence of death passed on, 101; behaviour of, at the place of execution, 102; is burned to death, 102, 103; the burial of, 103; a homily on, by Mar Jacob, 105, etc.; account of the martyrdom of, by Simon Metaphrastes, 146-149.

Hananiah, Michael, and Azariah, in the fiery furnace, compared with Habib, 106, 107.

Headbands, royal, 22, 24.

Herod the Great, the trouble between Abgar and, 150.

Herod the tetrarch, his quarrel with Aretas,—its cause, 153.

KINGS allowed to stand before the altar with the guides of the church, 43.

LENT, appointed by the apostles, 39.

Licinius the emperor, persecution under, 91, 92.

Luke, wrote the Acts, 49.

Lysanias seizes Sharbil, and carries him away to trial, 61; examines, tortures, and puts to death Sharbil, 62, etc.; Barsamya accused before, and examined, 81, etc.; Habib accused to, 91, 92; arrests Habib's family and others, 92; examines Habib, tortures, and condemns him to death, 96-101.

MAN, the Christians taunted for worshipping a, which they deny, 113, 114.

Marath Mary, goes daily to worship at Golgotha and the sepulchre,—the Jews strive to hinder, 133, 134.

Marinus, Abgar sends envoys to, 154.

Mar Jacob, a homily of, on Habib the martyr, 105, etc.; a canticle of, on Edessa, 129, 130; extracts from homilies of, 135.

Martyrs of Edessa, 114.

Medzpine, rebuilt by Sanadroug, 162.

Ministry, the Christian, in Edessa, the purity of, 33.

Months, the Syrian, 163.

Musonius, governor of Antioch, Guria and Shamuna tried, tortured, and put to death by, 139, etc.

NARSES, or Nersch, king of Assyria, sends to Abgar to inquire about Addæus—Abgar's reply, 26; letter of Abgar to, 159.

Nero, the emperor, commands Simon Cephas to be apprehended, and crucified with his head downwards, 54, 55; abandoned his empire, 55.

ORDINATION, in various countries, whence received, 46-48; the descent of that of the bishops of Edessa traced, 89, 90.

PALUT, made elder by Addæus, 29; ordained to the priesthood by Serapion, bishop of Antioch, 34, 35.

Persecution, the effect of, on the primitive church, 46.

Prayer, the power of, 126.

ROME, the population of, demand that all strangers shall be expelled from—the extraordinary result, 79, 80.

SANADROUG, son of Abgar, his apostasy and cruelty, 160; murder of Abgar's children by, and reign of, 161; rebuilds the city of Medzpine, 162; origin of his name, 162, 163.

Scriptures, apostolic arrangements respecting the reading of, in the assemblies, 40.

Serpent, the, crushed by the Son of God, 127.

Shamuna. [See *Guria and Shamuna*.]

Sharbil, the chief of the idol priests in Edessa, interesting account of his conversion, 57-60; converts multitudes, 60, 61; seized and carried away by Lysanias to be tried, 61; trial of, 61-65; scourged and imprisoned, 65; again brought before the judge, 65; caused to be suspended by his right hand, 66; tortured—his heroic endurance, 68, 69, 70, 71, 73, 74; sentence pronounced on, and executed, 76-78; the sister of, catches his blood, and is forthwith put to death, 78.

Simeon Metaphrastes, 136.

Simon Cephas, the teaching of, in Rome, 49-53; contest with and triumph over Simon the sorcerer—raises to life a dead man, 53,

54; the glad reception given, 54; seized by Nero, and ordered to be crucified, 54, 55.

Son of God, the, Christ owned as, 113; crushes the serpent, 127; espoused the church to Himself with His blood, 127.

THADDÆUS, or Addæus, sent by the Apostle Thomas to Abgar, king of Edessa, 6, 8; introduced to Abgar—their first interview, 9, 10; heals Abgar and Abdu, 12; refuses the gifts of Abgar, 13; relates the wonderful works of Christ to Abgar and his court, 13; preaches to Abgar, etc., 14; Abgar offers him help in his work, 21; replies to questions of the chief men, about Christ, 22, 23; builds a church in Edessa, 22; builds churches in the villages, 28; falls sick, and appoints Aggæus guide and ruler in his stead, 29; address of, to the nobles who had embraced Christianity, 29–31; his death, and mourning for, 31, 32; various extracts from the teaching of, 131; further statements respecting the mission and work of, 156, etc.

Theotecna, Habib the deacon delivers himself up to, who tries to persuade him to flee, 93, 94; accused of this to the governor, he denies the charge, 95.

Tiberius, Abgar's letter to, respecting the Jews who crucified Jesus, and the reply of, 26–28, 157, 158; another letter of Abgar to, 158, 159.

THE END.

MURRAY AND GIBB, EDINBURGH,
PRINTERS TO HER MAJESTY'S STATIONERY OFFICE.

www.ingramcontent.com/pod-product-compliance
Lightning Source LLC
Chambersburg PA
CBHW020303170426
43202CB00008B/484